ENGLISH COUNTRY CHURCHES

ENGLISH COUNTRY CHURCHES

DERRY BRABBS

INTRODUCTION BY

NIGEL NICOLSON

CASSELLPAPERBACKS

First published in 1985 by George Weidenfeld & Nicolson Ltd

This paperback edition first published in 2002 by
Cassell Paperbacks, Cassell & Co
Wellington House, 125 Strand
London, WC2R 0BB

Distributed in the United States of America by
Sterling Publishing Co., Inc.
387 Park Avenue South,
New York, NY 10016-8810

British Library Cataloguing-in-Publication Data
A catalogue record for this book is available from
the British Library

ISBN 1-84188-177-5

Designed by Helen Lewis
Filmset by Keyspools, Golborne, Lancashire
Colour separations by Newsele Litho Ltd
Printed and bound in Italy by L.E.G.O., Vicenza

Half-title page: St Mary the Virgin, Painswick, Gloucestershire
Title page: Holy Trinity, Bosham, West Sussex

CONTENTS

ST EDITH
COATES-BY-STOW, LINCOLNSHIRE

The tiny church of St Edith contrasts starkly with its near neighbour, the monumental Anglo-Saxon and Norman church at Stow (page 31), but those who visit this very old building will be rewarded by that special feeling of the past that seems to linger in the smaller rural churches.

The Norman south doorway still displays its bold dog-tooth moulding, but some of the original windows have been enlarged or blocked up. The simple rustic interior with its brick floor is greatly enhanced by a Perpendicular carved oak rood screen, which retains its loft and tympanum. Although a certain amount of restoration has been necessary, traces of the original painted figures are visible.

The inspiration for this book came from the work of the Poet Laureate, Sir John Betjeman, whose love of England was so vividly reflected in his writing, particularly in his collection of church poems. It was that affectionate and often humourous tribute to an ancient institution that led me on a voyage of discovery round the country from the Scottish border to Land's End tracking down some of the oldest, smallest, remotest and most picturesque churches in England.

Fortified churches of the north, built to withstand harsh winters and marauding Scots, black-and-white half-timbered buildings of Cheshire, sumptuous 'wool' churches of the Cotswolds and Suffolk, elegant Perpendicular towers of Somerset, tough granite churches of Cornwall, we tend to take them all for granted as a natural part of the landscape. I have always been happy to use the solid towers and soaring spires as integral components of a carefully composed photograph, but never gave the buildings themselves much thought. To produce a definitive list of the 'best' churches would be impossible; what follows is a purely personal selection, a 'celebration' of fine craftsmanship and human endeavour that does not dwell too heavily on architectural technicalities and jargon.

I am indebted to Nigel Nicolson for his introduction, and my grateful thanks are also due to my editor, Felicity Luard.

Derry Brabbs

INTRODUCTION
BY NIGEL NICOLSON

ST MARY
KINGSTON ST MARY,
SOMERSET

One of the highly regarded 'Taunton group' of churches, Kingston St Mary differs from some of its neighbours by being built of sandstone. The architect did, however, use golden Ham Hill limestone for those parts bearing the greatest carved detail, mainly on the tower, and it blends perfectly with the New Red sandstone. When lit by the early morning or late evening sun the church radiates a great warmth of colour.

The church originated early in the thirteenth century, but in common with many others in the region was enlarged and refashioned in the Perpendicular style late in the fifteenth. Compared with other Somerset towers, Kingston is not spectacularly tall or as elaborately decorated, but its feeling of strength, its perfectly balanced proportions and the elegantly spired crown combine to make it one of the most successful.

The medieval churches of England represent a phenomenal achievement. At the Reformation there were some 46,000 of them, in addition to thousands of monastic churches, cathedrals, chapels and chantries, all raised during a few centuries by a population that numbered little more than the present population of New Zealand. About half of them survive in a more or less recognizable state. The other half were lost or replaced in later centuries, particularly the nineteenth, for the Victorians were the greatest church-builders since the Normans – but their churches were built mainly to serve the needs of the expanding cities, and lie outside the scope of this book.

We are concerned here with the churches of villages and small towns, admirably illustrated and described by Derry Brabbs in the pages that follow. He devotes a section of his book to isolated churches that through accidents of history like the Black Death, or the whims of great landowners, appear divorced from their present congregations. But in the main his churches lie in or near the centres of small communities. A church is the village hub. It is the first building that a child will set down in arranging a toy town; he will want it, instinctively, to be medieval, and when he or she marries, the older the church, the better. The church is our main link with the remoter past, and though it contains the most museum-worthy objects to be found in most villages, it is by no means a museum. It was built for prayer; it is still used for prayer. It is the largest building in a parish, in many of them the only communal building, probably the only one built of stone, the only one with a predominantly vertical accent, the only one that emits, unmistakably, its own sound, and the only one to be free of a television aerial.

It is a pity that the word 'sentimental' has become unusable except as a term of disapproval and that no other has replaced it, because it exactly expresses the emotion aroused by an old church, and sentiment is nothing to be sneezed at. The church represents, even for those who are more often church-visitors than church-goers, a continuity of local history, and a condensation of our national history, which is equalled only by the few old houses that we are permitted to enter – but they are evidence of a personal taste and way of life, while the church reflects society as a whole. If we had no such visual reminders of the past, the past would scarcely exist for us, for not many people have much knowledge of, or feeling for, their progenitors beyond their great-grandfathers. The church and its churchyard literally contain the village's past inhabitants, their tombs and humbler gravestones recording who they were, when they lived, by whom they were loved, and often what they achieved and what sort of people they were. The church itself is an irreplaceable record of how men built, of their technical and artistic inventiveness, of their self-denial for a communal and religious cause, of an architectural genius that we have lost, and of an intensity and universality of faith that one day we may recover.

To enter such a church alone is as great a spiritual experience as to form part of a congregation worshipping in it, indeed often greater, for the solitude, emptiness, solidity, permanence, grace, cleanliness and the very smell of it induce reflections and a sense of repose that one experiences in no other way, except in a beautiful wood in spring or on a mountain top. Imagine visiting with equivalent emotion any other place of public assembly emptied of people – a railway station, a supermarket, an airport or even a theatre or concert-hall! All such places are replaceable, and few of them would be for long regretted. But a medieval church, like a great house, can never be replaced or imitated. When the Victorians attempted it, they created something quite different in feeling. We build modern churches, but almost all are mean in comparison to the great structures of the Middle Ages, and the tricks we play with new shapes, ground plans and materials only reveal our uncertainty of what a church should be like, and hence what it is for.

Consider the poverty, sickness and ignorance of the men who created these old buildings, maintained them, embellished them and constantly added to them in a slowly developing style. Their whole building effort was put into their churches. Their own habitations remained as crude and bereft of comforts as a village in Swaziland. Their lives were hard and brutal. They were persecuted by their landlords, sometimes by the Church itself. The church was their only refuge, materially and spiritually. For the common people it was their only luxury. So they built luxuriously, helped and encouraged by their cathedral city, their local priests and liege lords, but it was basically a communal effort. For a few it provided paid employment – masons, sculptors, carpenters, painters, quarrymen and carters – just as it did (Plutarch records) for the builders of the Parthenon in fifth-century Athens. But most of the work was done by untrained men in what time they could spare from their labours in the fields.

There were no architects in our modern sense. Master masons roughly drew out the plan and elevations, and master carpenters erected the scaffolding and built the roof. These were the professionals who travelled from village to village, but those rough stone walls that still stand were the work of simple men attempting a considerable feat of engineering. Even the master masons of the earlier period of church-building had little idea what stresses were at work on such a building, what load per square inch they were placing on the bases of their piers and walls, and they could make mistakes – especially on an unstable soil – hoping that the walls would find a natural angle of repose, even if some ended up aslant. There were not even fixed standards of measurement. Medieval builders lacked something so basic as a tape measure. They had the use of pulley-and-rope, but a workman must have known that every fresh stone he laid might bring the whole structure down. They built in stone because it was more impressive and enduring, and where no local stone was available, it had to be carted or dragged on sledges over long distances on poor tracks or brought by water, sometimes from France. The huge balks of timbers needed to span the roof presented the same difficulties. The stone was shaped by axe and chisel, the wood by saw and adze. It was a colossal task to assemble and prepare the materials, and a risky one to build with them.

Yet people persisted with astonishing determination. They built their churches far larger than the local population could ever fill, partly for the greater glory of God and to give room for impressive processions, partly to rival the neighbouring village, and partly because the church in the Middle Ages was not only a place for worship, but for communal meetings of all kinds, including plays, feasts and dances, and for refuge in times of trouble (church towers originated in Saxon times as lookout posts). Churches were built in astounding (for us almost embarrassing) profusion. When it would have been easy for villagers to walk a mile or two to a central church, as they did daily to distant fields, every hamlet must have its own. From the tower of my village church I can see a dozen others. In another part of Kent with which I am familiar, Romney Marsh, the population was so sparse that even today there are churches without houses near them, and not all the churches built still exist. There was no local stone: it was dragged from Maidstone, or ferried from Normandy. The nearest trees grew six miles away. These graceful buildings were erected despite the dangers and setbacks inevitable in a low-lying land threatened by flood from the rivers and the sea. What is the explanation? It has been said that as the marshland was gradually reclaimed, each fresh 'inning' was marked by a church, to provide a new centre for habitation, a vertical element where all else was flat, and a pointer for strangers coming from a distance. But it was more than that. It was an expression of confidence in a future that was expected to be less arduous than the present, and an enduring memorial to the strength of people's beliefs. The same motives are evident in every part of the country.

Apart from the first chapter, the photographs in this book are not arranged chronologically to explain the different periods of church architecture, but more imaginatively to illustrate their different qualities and situations. Following Derry Brabbs's example I shall not attempt to trace the story of ecclesiastical building from the earliest times, except by drawing attention to the sudden change that occurred in the fourteenth century and produced one of the most spectacular and beautiful styles known to architectural history, and one exclusively English, which we call, rather dully, the Perpendicular, simply because its main emphasis was vertical.

We must remember that people began to build like this soon after the Black Death, which killed a third of the population and left the survivors among the peasantry desperately poor and shaken. Yet this low point in the nation's fortunes was the period when men rebuilt or altered all but the humblest of their parish churches, and built new ones of astonishing audacity and extravagance. Many of the great ornamental towers and spires date from this period. Huge windows were inserted at the east and west ends and along each side of the nave. Often the nave or chancel was lengthened. The invention of the flying buttress and its heavy pinnacles made possible the construction of thinner walls, and these structural devices became additional ornaments. Aisles were built outwards to enlarge the church, and chapels and chantries were formed within it or added to the outside. Much of this work involved the risk of weakening old walls by replacing huge areas of stone by glass and delicate tracery, or by breaking through them to create slender arcades or more magnificent doorways. You can often see above these new arches the original stonework of the Norman exterior wall, and what seems to us quite natural and all of one piece was an astonishing feat of structural engineering. Not many parish churches could afford to replace timber roofs by stone vaulting, but that they were quite capable of it is shown by several of the great churches in Somerset, the Cotswolds and East Anglia. Whenever possible the new generation of builders would adopt the High Gothic device of running the slender flutings of the columns in an unbroken sweep to shape the angles of the roof, omitting the capitals. These innovations transformed the churches, which in early medieval times must have been dark and cold, into airy sun-filled cages. The masonry formed its own decoration. It was the loveliest ecclesiastical style ever devised, great stability being achieved with the appearance of great fragility. Church architecture grew better and better as the fourteenth century advanced to the fifteenth, and reached its supreme glory not only in King's College, St George's at Windsor and the Henry VII chapel in Westminster Abbey, but in lesser churches like Steeple Ashton in Wiltshire, Cirencester, Boxgrove Priory in West Sussex and Sherborne Abbey.

The whole explosive process was halted by the Reformation at the moment when it could achieve nothing finer, and secular architecture took over to create wonderful houses like Longleat, Hardwick and Montacute, which owe nothing to ecclesiastical building. It is not often realized that there has never been, in any country, so rapid, so well-timed in one sense, so revolutionary a switch in a country's architectural style. Nothing like our High Gothic is found in the rest of Europe, nothing like the Elizabethan country house. It was a period, straddling less than a hundred years, when we reached the peak of our inventiveness and skills, first in cathedrals and churches, then in capacious houses that boxed together, within shells of outstanding novelty and beauty, rooms large and small that still express our ideal of noble living.

Church-building did not stop with the Reformation, but there was a long pause after it, because the country was amply, even over churched, and when building began again in the late seventeenth and eighteenth centuries, it was in quite a different manner, more florid, squarer, lower and classical. We must be grateful that the Georgians did not modernize the Gothic churches as they did old manor houses and castles. When they made changes it was in an eighteenth-century version of the medieval, not in imitation of it but in full sympathy with it. They added their own tombs and chapels, but kept the old ones, the windows and the font. What they added as furniture was wholly admirable – pulpits, box pews and galleries in polished woods, like those that survive in the churches at Wanstead, Essex, or Langton-by-Spilsby in Lincolnshire, but much of it was swept away by the Victorians because they believed it to be out of character.

They were wrong. A work of art or excellent craftsmanship of any period is never out of place in any church, and the saddest part of the long story of our churches is that we are contributing to them so little that future generations will look upon with pleasure. Mean wall tablets arranged like stamps in an album; electrical and heating appliances with their beastly wires and pipes that in a private house would be decently concealed, 'all in the name of economy and efficiency', as John Betjeman wrote, 'and none in the name of reverence'; tatty children's corners and carpets of too gorgeous a blue – in these ways we are in danger of trivializing a great inheritance.

However, these things are ephemeral and remediable. Of far greater importance is that we think these churches worth preserving and using. We have this incomparable evidence of how people built in past ages, how they altered what they found, and therefore how they thought. We are subconsciously influenced by these surroundings in our own manner of thinking and worshipping. You can be married at a chancel step where countless others were married before and with the same ritual, christen your baby in a Norman font, sit in the seat where a squire sat centuries ago and hear the same words as he heard, read from the same lectern, often from the same Bible. The symbols of our religion, in spite of the change in creed, are unchanged since Saxon times. The vestments of visiting Bishops are reproduced in stained glass over your head, as they are in the recumbent effigies of their predecessors in the cathedrals. Looking upwards at a great arch or clerestory or hammer-beam roof you may imagine the skill and daring of the man who made it, and around you read the lapidary inscriptions proclaiming the virtues of a man or woman who stands for thousands who worshipped in this church and are now forgotten.

All this was achieved gradually and never mechanically. There were imitations and repetitions from church to church as a journeyman mason carried his own ideas or other craftsmen's across the country. But what is remarkable about our churches is that within a given formula and tradition – the basic arrangement of tower, nave, aisles, chapels, porch and chancel – each church has a different shape and personality, so that each combines familiarity with surprise, like a garden with its different vistas and groupings of well-known flowers. The pleasure that this book has given me is that it reproduces this variety by sampling it, and introduced me to many churches that I shall probably never see with my own eyes.

ST MICHAEL
DUNTISBOURNE ROUSE, GLOUCESTERSHIRE

Gloriously situated on a steep valley side near a remote hamlet, St Michael's embodies all the charms of our ancient rural churches. The setting is matched by an attractive exterior with a small, saddleback tower, and by a simple and unspoilt interior.

When viewed from the side the steepness of the site can be fully appreciated; it enabled the Normans to put a crypt beneath the chancel when building on to the existing church. The tiny crypt was originally approached from the chancel, but that entrance is now blocked, the only access being down steep steps from the churchyard.

Four very old misericords are an unusual find in such a small church. Possibly they came from a monastic building such as Cirencester Abbey after the Dissolution. Inside the nave are simple, wood-panelled box pews, a strong chancel arch and a Norman font. Electricity was not installed until 1960, services before then being held in the subdued glow of candlelight.

There were two distinct influences on early Christianity and church-building in England: St Augustine, who landed in Kent in AD 597 and the Celtic missionaries from Iona who, led by St Aidan, settled on Lindisfarne, an island off the Northumbrian coast, in AD 635.

St Augustine started to build stone churches patterned on the Roman basilica with a rounded apse, the majority in Kent, a notable exception being Bradwell-on-Sea in Essex, one of the best examples still surviving. The Celtic churches were generally tall and narrow, with box-like naves leading to square-ended chancels. Most of these original churches were built of timber from the forests that covered large parts of the country, a material that was not as suitable as stone for constructing curves and semicircles. The only Saxon timber church remaining is at Greensted in Essex; huge vertical oak logs still form the walls of the nave.

Until the famous Synod of Whitby in AD 664, the Celtic and Roman missions followed their own separate teachings and rites – even the Church calendars differed. The meeting at Whitby was to establish which body should be followed in unity, the result being a rejection of the Celtic Church in favour of the Roman. The Celtic religion then drifted out of England back to the remoter parts of Britain.

We owe much to the Venerable Bede (673–735) for his writings about the formative years of the English Church. His *Ecclesiastical History of the English People* provides a graphic account of the lives and work of the early saints and Saxon bishops; tells of church-builders and church-building; and gives valuable information about daily life that archaeological evidence alone could not supply.

Ironically, despite the dominance of the Roman Church, the parish churches that grew up over the years largely favoured the Celtic design of the square-ended chancel with a large east window, a feature that probably dated back to pagan worship when the altar and priest had to be fully lit by the morning sun.

Around the year AD 800 the Vikings increased the severity of their annual raids, continuing to plunder the east coast and pushing far into Mercia (the Midlands) by sailing their long ships up the navigable rivers. Many of the original timber churches were burnt by the raiders and, as stone became more widely used in construction, towers gradually increased in number, offering the only safe refuge to the population. A large quantity of these are standing today, incorporated into church-building of later periods. Saxon towers are characterized by their height, slender proportions and by their huge blocks of rough-hewn masonry. Kirk Hammerton in Yorkshire is a perfect example.

The relatively peaceful period of fifty years or so before the Conquest produced much of the fine Anglo-Saxon art and architecture that is still visible around the country today. Despite the apparent roughness of some of the exterior stonework of their churches, Saxon masons were capable of great quality and finesse – the crossing and transepts of Stow in Lincolnshire provide illustrations of soaring grace and elegance.

After the Conquest there followed a spate of building by the new feudal lords, knocking down the old Saxon wood churches and rebuilding in stone. Many of these simple, rural Norman churches no longer exist, but there are survivors, usually in remote areas untouched by developers and restorers. Winterborne Tomson in Dorset is a particularly good example of the aisleless nave and apsidal chancel plan that was common at that time.

Larger churches of the early Norman period tended to be rather austere and unornamented, but gradually, around 1130, there began the marvellous period of Romanesque carving that produced such masterpieces as Kilpeck in Hereford and Barfreston in Kent. Chancel arches throughout the country were decorated with the familiar chevron patterning, often up to six layers deep, and the hitherto plain capitals became more ornately sculpted; arches, doorways and windows all began to show the results of fast-developing skills and techniques.

Although we can easily see the work of the sculptors, there is one aspect of the Norman church that is now missing – the wall-paintings that covered the insides of most churches are lost forever, apart from a handful of rare exceptions. Wall-painting went on right through the Middle Ages, it was a way of getting over the biblical message to a mainly illiterate population; as with television today, graphic colour pictures speak far more vividly than words.

ST MARY
LASTINGHAM, NORTH YORKSHIRE

Marooned on a sea of bracken high on the North Yorkshire Moors, the small village of Lastingham possesses one of the most moving religious treasures to be found anywhere in the country. Encompassed within the parish church of St Mary is an eleventh-century crypt, a complete church in itself and a shrine to St Cedd, who is buried by the altar.

Lastingham's crypt is unique in that it has a nave, aisles and an apsidal chancel, the nave being particularly impressive due to the heavy vaulting and the great size of its pillars. Work was begun on the crypt by Abbot Stephen in 1078, who built it on the site of the stone church that formed part of a monastery founded by Cedd in AD 659, and which had been sacked by marauding Vikings.

Stephen had sought permission from William the Conqueror to rebuild the monastery, but, having finished the crypt and started on what would have been a great abbey church, he took his monks to safer territory in York and there founded St Mary's Abbey. Stephen's plans for Lastingham were never to be fulfilled; the present church was eventually finished in 1228.

ST MARY AND ST DAVID

KILPECK, HEREFORD AND WORCESTER

Kilpeck is renowned for the quality and intricacy of its carvings, which are surprisingly well preserved due to the unusual hardness of the local red sandstone. Many churches of this material weather very quickly, but here the elaborate craftsmanship is still etched almost as clearly as when completed, in the middle of the twelfth century.

Considered to be one of the finest remaining examples of late Romanesque style, Kilpeck follows the Norman three-cell pattern of nave, chancel and apse. If any one feature of this remarkable church has to be singled out it must surely be the south doorway. The two arches over the door are filled with a strange collection of animals, birds and other creatures, suggesting a portrayal of the Creation. The door jambs apparently depict Eden, with man being tempted by the fruit from the Tree of Life and the ensuing battle between good and evil.

More than seventy grotesque carvings form the corbel table that runs round the outside of the church. Many are human heads, horribly haunting, others are symbols of the chase, such as falcons, wild boar and deer.

The name Kilpeck is derived from the 'Cell of Pedic', a church having occupied the same site long before the Normans came.

ST NICHOLAS

STUDLAND, DORSET

It seems appropriate that the dedication of this coastal Norman church should be to the patron saint of sailors. Considered to be a very fine example of early Norman architecture, St Nicholas's replaced an earlier, Saxon church of very similar size. The Danes were responsible for the near destruction of the original building and caused much similar damage throughout the region until defeated by King Alfred in AD 877.

The church consists of a nave, tower space and chancel. The tower was never completed by the Norman builders, possibly due to concern about the feasibility of such a structure surviving on virtually no foundations. This decision was vindicated in 1881 when a substantial rescue operation was mounted. Deep trenches were dug round the tower and sanctuary so that the walls could be underpinned with bricks and concrete. The original foundations were found to consist of rough pieces of sandstone and clay, causing the restorers to wonder why a collapse had not occurred before.

The excavations gave further evidence of the age of the church as different burial levels were unearthed. Christian Saxon graves were discovered and pre-Christian 'cists' of local flint.

ST ANDREW
GREENSTED, ESSEX

St Andrew's is the only surviving example of a Saxon timber-framed church and has been scientifically dated to AD 845, making it the oldest wooden church in the world.

There was a church on this site before the present one and it is likely that the original building was founded on a Celtic pre-Christian place of worship. There had been several attempts to convert Essex, but it was not until St Cedd established his cathedral at Bradwell-on-Sea that Christianity was finally accepted here.

The Saxon nave is remarkable for the huge vertical oak logs that form the walls. These were tongued-and-grooved for draughtproofing and fixed in place with wooden pins, no metal nails were used at all in the construction. The roof was thatched and there were no windows, holes bored in the walls provided ventilation and burning torches gave light.

There have been many additions to the original church through the years, the most extensive being during the reign of Henry VII, around 1500. The Tudors rebuilt the chancel, formed the porch, replaced the thatched roof with tiles and included three dormer windows.

Although now modernized, the timbered interior exudes great warmth and manages to retain its feeling of the past.

ST PETER-ON-THE-WALL
BRADWELL-ON-SEA, ESSEX

One of the earliest surviving churches in the country, St Peter-on-the-Wall sits completely alone on the shore of the Blackwater estuary. There is no road to the chapel so visitors must use the same track that carried the Romans inland from the third-century fort of Othona, the stones from which were used by St Cedd to build his Christian outpost over 300 years later in AD 654. St Peter-on-the-Wall is so named because it is sited on the main gateway of the fort's west wall.

St Cedd sailed from Lindisfarne at the request of Sigbert, a recently converted Saxon King, and built his church in the township named Ythancestrir, which was centred on the old Roman station. St Peter's originally consisted of nave, apse and west porch, but only the nave remains. The extent of the apse has been traced and outlined in concrete during excavations.

The church was certainly used for centuries after St Cedd's death and probably became the chapel of ease to the parish church, which was built further inland. During the late eighteenth century St Peter-on-the-Wall was used as a barn and remained as such until handed back to the Church some 150 years later. A sensitive restoration was carried out leaving the building virtually unaltered and without furnishings, the chapel was then reconsecrated on 22 June 1920.

ST LAURENCE
BRADFORD-ON-AVON, WILTSHIRE

The complete Saxon church of St Laurence is a relatively recent 'discovery', having been used over the centuries for non-religious purposes. It may well be that it ceased to be a place of worship when the neighbouring parish church was built in the twelfth century. There is no record of it in the Domesday book and it is referred to as the 'Skull House' in old sets of deeds. This could mean it was used as a charnel house and would explain why the base fabric of the building remained unaltered.

There were, however, many alterations inside, the nave became a school and the chancel a cottage, the chancel arch having been pulled down to construct a chimney. Fortunately all the stones were kept enabling the arch to be rebuilt during restoration. It was the uncovering of two carved angels during repair work in 1856 that led the vicar, Canon Jones, to start tracing the history of the building in the belief that it may have been an ancient church. Subsequent research in the Bodleian Library, Oxford, led him to passages from William of Malmesbury, dated *circa* 1125, which mentioned 'a little church which Aldhelm built to the name of the most blessed Laurence'.

Although the original church was founded by St Aldhelm about AD 700, a later rebuilding must have taken place; expert examination of the stones reveal tool marks from both Saxon and early Norman periods.

ST ANDREW
WINTERBORNE TOMSON, DORSET

St Andrew's is one of the rare surviving examples of a single-cell Norman church with apse dating from about 1090. Churches like this sprang up all over the country as the new lords took possession of lands and estates granted to them after the Conquest, but most of these buildings have disappeared or been swallowed up by reconstruction at a later time.

Winterborne Tomson is one of a group of hamlets all bearing the Winterborne prefix. The church stands next to a manor house and was disused for a long period until well restored in the 1930s in memory of Thomas Hardy. The last major work carried out prior to that was in the eighteenth century, when Georgian fittings were installed. The plastered wagon roof and faded oak box pews blend perfectly in this simple whitewashed interior. There is a gallery that was formed from the medieval rood loft, although some of the wood is now showing signs of decay. Despite its remoteness St Andrew's is well cared for by the Redundant Churches Fund and services are still held from time to time.

HOLY TRINITY
BOSHAM, WEST SUSSEX

The ancient waterside church at Bosham is steeped in history and legend. Romantically set on the edge of Chichester harbour, Holy Trinity appears in the Bayeaux Tapestry, since it was from here that the ill-fated Harold Godwin, later King Harold, set sail to Normandy in 1064.

Holy Trinity is built on the site of an ancient Roman basilica, the present church dating from about 1020. There is a possibility that King Canute was the founder of Bosham church. Legend has it that he lived nearby and that his eight-year-old daughter was buried in the church after a drowning accident. Weight was given to the legend when in 1865 a coffin containing the remains of a child was discovered below the floor of the nave during rebuilding work. The coffin has been dated to Canute's time.

Beneath the chapel of All Hallows in the south aisle is a crypt, which is thought to occupy the site of Dicul's cell. He was an Irish monk who established a place of worship here in the seventh century, but, according to the Venerable Bede, achieved little success: 'None of the natives of the country cared either to imitate their life or to listen to their preaching.'

ST NICHOLAS
BARFRESTON, KENT

St Nicholas's is a small, two-cell Norman church of nave and chancel, separated by a zigzag patterned arch. Considered to be the finest example of its period in Kent, Barfreston's main attraction is the wealth of elaborate carving both inside and out. The south doorway could be compared to the similar example at Kilpeck in Hereford. Careful scrutiny will reveal strange images: Samson opening a lion's jaws; a bear playing a harp; a monkey with a rabbit over its shoulder riding a goat, and many more. In the centre of the tympanum sits Our Lord, hand raised in blessing. A more unusual feature is the large wheel window at the east end, again surrounded by intricate craftsmanship. The whole church is a tribute to the masons who worked the Caen stone late in the twelfth century and many similarities have been found between the styles employed here and in some notable churches in France.

St Nicholas's was restored by Edward Blore in 1840 but remained basically unaltered. One slightly unusual thing is that since there is no tower or belfry, the church bell hangs in a nearby yew.

ST MARY
SOMPTING, WEST SUSSEX

Sompting is renowned for its distinctive tower, capped with a Rhenish helm. St Mary's is the only example of this German design in England and the tower is almost certainly pre-Conquest, probably about AD 1050. It is possible that there were other similar towers, but additions and rebuilding over the centuries have left very few such pieces of Saxon work untouched.

The nave and chancel were rebuilt by the Templars when they were granted the church in 1154. They also added a separate chapel for themselves, which now forms the south transept. No arch separates nave and chancel, but the tower arch carries some fairly good Saxon carving. Work of a much higher standard can be found in strips of foliage on the walls.

There are various other carvings from Saxon and later periods, but the undoubted glories of Sompting are its tower and its superb position: a downland slope overlooking the sea.

ST MARY
BREAMORE, HAMPSHIRE

Breamore is an unusually large Saxon church with a central tower, dating back to about AD 1000. It was a forerunner of the cruciform plan church that became so popular in the Middle Ages, although here the transepts do not reach the full height of the nave and have very little depth. The exterior walls, built from whole flints, would originally have been covered by plaster.

Over the tower arch that leads into the south transept, or chapel, is an old Saxon inscription, HER SWUTELATH SEO GECWYDRAEDNES THE, which means, 'Here the Covenant becomes manifest to thee.' Analysis of the carved letters has dated the inscription to the latter part of the reign of Ethelred II, 979–1016.

Breamore is also notable for the remains of a Saxon rood, unfortunately badly defaced after the Reformation. It is now protected by the south porch, where it hangs, and relief figures of Our Lady and St John can be seen amid traces of the fifteenth-century painted background.

St Mary's has three Mass clocks, a simple kind of sundial often found carved on the walls of the earliest churches. They were used to tell the time for services, particularly Mass, but are seldom found complete, the gnomon (pointer) is usually missing.

HEATH CHAPEL
SHROPSHIRE

This tiny undedicated Norman church lies hidden high in the Shropshire hills to the north of Ludlow. Many of these parochial chapels were built around 1100 to enable the inhabitants from the remoter parts of the large Saxon parishes to receive ministrations from the Church.

No churchyards are found with these simple places of worship, the right of burial being rigorously enforced by the Mother church, but all had fonts to ensure that no infant died without baptism. The parishioners were obliged to attend the parish church on its saint's day and other major festivals, whatever distance was involved.

The inside walls of the church are covered with crumbling plaster revealing distinct traces of paintings from different periods. Efforts are being made to restore the best sections, a fourteenth-century St George has been uncovered on the south wall and seventeenth-century cartouche paintings on the north. The interior is quite dark, lit only by the original Norman slits. The furnishings are a mixture of seventeenth-century box pews and tiny benches.

ST MARY
STOW, LINCOLNSHIRE

St Mary's is a huge, powerful Anglo-Saxon and Norman building of cathedral-like proportions, seemingly out of place in this remote village. The largest remaining church of the period, it also retains the original true cruciform plan with transepts and central tower.

The history of the church starts long before the Conquest; two earlier buildings were pillaged, one by the Danes, the other by King Canute. The oldest parts of the current church are the transepts and crossing, which are dominated by tall and surprisingly elegant Saxon arches. The builders were perhaps fortunate that Stow lies on a belt of particularly fine oolitic limestone, the quality of the stone making it easier to work.

The Normans took over the construction and Remigius, first Bishop of Lincoln, was responsible for the truly impressive nave. The chancel followed early in the twelfth century, but underwent a fairly dramatic, though sensitive, restoration in the 1850s under J. L. Pearson.

ST GREGORY
KIRKDALE, NORTH YORKSHIRE

St Gregory's Minster is situated in wooded country on the fringe of the North Yorkshire Moors. The most impressive feature of this Saxon church is a sundial over the south porch, the most complete specimen still existing in England. A clear inscription on the stone face of the dial provides information enabling the church to be dated to around AD 1060. The translation informs us that 'St Gregory's Minster, in a broken down state, was bought by Orm Gamal's son and was then rebuilt.' This proves the existence of a previous church, which may well have been connected with the monastery founded at nearby Lastingham in AD 659 by the much travelled missionary brothers, St Cedd and St Chad.

The oldest part of St Gregory's is the nave where there is a typical tall, narrow Saxon entrance arch. The aisle was added around 1200, but the tower and chancel were rebuilt in their present form as late as the nineteenth century. Unfortunately this gives the exterior a strange, slightly unbalanced look, but even so nothing can detract from the beauty of the original work.

ST MARY THE VIRGIN
STAINBURN, NORTH YORKSHIRE

The windswept churchyard offers a wide, dramatic view over Lower Wharfedale. St Mary the Virgin is set apart from the tiny village of Stainburn and represents a simple Norman country church.

The medieval porch shelters a plain Norman doorway, and the gold-tinted stone of the chancel arch is also undecorated. Finer masonry work can be seen on the font with its interlaced arcading.

St Mary's windows vary in style from the narrow original slits to a strange triangular-headed one from the seventeenth century. The interior is furnished with long, simple oak pews and a seventeenth-century pulpit.

ST JOHN THE BAPTIST
KIRK HAMMERTON, NORTH YORKSHIRE

Formerly dedicated to St Quentin, the original Saxon church now forms the tower and south aisle of the present one. The north wall was removed about 1150 to make way for an extra aisle. That work was probably well executed unlike the heavy-handed enlargements that followed in the nineteenth century, the final restoration being by C. H. Fowler in 1891.

Enough of the chancel arch remains to give an impression of the pure Saxon work inside the church, but it is the exterior that really takes the eye. When viewed from the south, most of the newer work is hidden by the original wall and tower so that the enormous, rough-hewn stones are all that can be seen. The Saxon windows have been replaced, but this in no way affects the pleasure gained from observing a marvellous piece of tenth-century building.

ST MARY THE VIRGIN
SEAHAM, COUNTY DURHAM

St Mary's has the appearance of a fugitive fleeing from the advancing pit heads and coking ovens but who, having reached the cliffs of the North Sea, can retreat no further. In fact the church was here long before the industry that now surrounds it. The nave is possibly as old as seventh or eighth century, some of the masonry having come from a nearby Roman signal station.

Three small, round-headed windows survive in the nave, while the thirteenth-century chancel has rounded lancets. St Mary's tower was added a little later than the chancel and all the exterior stonework now has the worn, eroded look that comes from exposure to smoke and a chemically polluted atmosphere.

All the box pews are still in place including those of the rector and squire, which are located in the chancel. A most careful and tasteful restoration of the church was carried out in 1913, leaving the interior unspoiled and still full of atmosphere.

The village of Seaham has disappeared, only the hall and former vicarage remaining intact. It is strange to think that Seaham has literary connections, for it was here, in an upstairs drawing room at Seaham Hall, that Lord Byron married Anne Milbanke in 1815. A copy of the marriage register is usually included with the guide provided for visitors to the church.

ST MICHAEL
ISEL, CUMBRIA

Isel church was built by the Normans in 1130 close to the wooded banks of the River Derwent. Translated, Derwent means 'oak river' and centuries ago the whole area was covered by dense forest. Travellers used the river courses and woodland tracks, and places of worship were often set up at intersections of these routes. There is evidence that this is such a site, since carved stones that predate the church by 200 years were found in the walls during restoration. One of these, the 'Triskele' stone, carries a three-armed symbol that was used by the earliest Christians.

St Michael's has an unusually large number of windows for its size, fifteen, varying from the original Norman slits to the large west window of 1878. There was once a tower, often a necessary defensive feature in churches built close to the border, but this has been replaced by the present belfry. Furnishings inside the church worth noting include the altar frontal, a beautiful piece of work incorporating material woven with Chinese gold, some of which fabric came from hangings used in Westminster Abbey for the coronation of Edward VII in 1902.

OUR LADY
SEATON DELAVAL,
NORTHUMBERLAND

The small Norman church of Our Lady was originally the private chapel of the Delaval family, built by Hubert Delaval and consecrated in 1102. It is located in the grounds of Seaton Delaval Hall, a Palladian mansion designed by Vanbrugh for Admiral George Delaval, and built in 1729. Experts consider this to be Vanbrugh's finest work, although ironically both he and the Admiral died before the project was completed.

Our Lady consists of nave, chancel and a later chancel extension, probably replacing the original Norman apse. Both chancel and apse arches remain intact and are identical in shape and decoration. They have roll and hollow mouldings with lines of zigzag carving around the outside.

There are two notable fourteenth-century effigies, a cross-legged knight, and a lady from some years later. Another outstanding feature is the series of eight stone panels containing shields bearing the Delaval and other arms from the fourteenth century.

ST ANDREW
BOLAM, NORTHUMBERLAND

Bolam was once a thriving village with a reputation for producing fine saddlery but is now deserted and abandoned. St Andrew's has survived and enjoys a beautiful location in the undulating landscape of Bolam Country Park.

The church is primarily noted for its late Saxon tower, tall and unbuttressed, with narrow, two-light bell openings above which are tiny single arches.

Most of the interior is dominated by Norman architecture, with a finely moulded chancel arch supported on pillars made up of three strong shafts with scalloped capitals. The arcade between nave and south aisle has rounded arches, but seemingly from a later date than the chancel arch. Thirteenth-century work appears round the south doorway and in the east part of the chancel, much of it readily identifiable by the distinctive dog-tooth decoration.

A stone effigy, sadly mutilated, represents a border knight, Robert de Raynes, who died in 1342. There are also a number of coffin lids incised with crosses and memorials to the Middleton family of Belsay, both inside the church and in the graveyard.

ST ANDREW
HEDDON-ON-THE-WALL, NORTHUMBERLAND

St Andrew's occupies a quiet corner away from the road that follows the line of Hadrian's Wall between Newcastle and Carlisle. The church has significant traces of Saxon work, exhibited by the long-and-short stonework, blocked doorways and windows. It originally had a rounded apse, which was replaced by a splendid Norman vaulted sanctuary when extensions were begun about AD 1155. This work was instigated by the monks from Blanchland Abbey who were granted lands around Heddon at that time, the church thus becoming part of their responsibility.

All the glass in the church, which includes a 'Jesse' window, is modern and was stained at the same time. Seven earlier windows had to be dismantled and the memorials and saints were incorporated into the new designs.

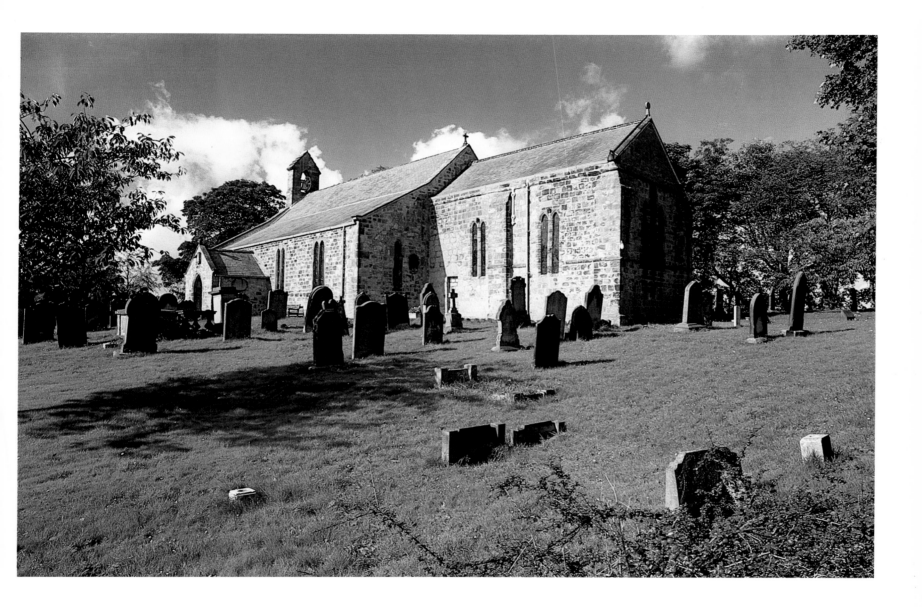

ST MICHAEL THE ARCHANGEL
KIRBY MALHAM, NORTH YORKSHIRE

Kirby Malham is situated just to the south of the great limestone amphitheatre of Malham Cove and close by the route of the Pennine Way. This is rough countryside, a characteristic that is reflected in its buildings.

St Michael's is fifteenth century and built of millstone grit, a tough north-country stone fit to fend off the Pennine winters. The style of architecture is known as Craven Perpendicular. Several churches in this region have similar characteristics, tending to be long, low buildings with solid towers.

St Michael's interior is not nearly so uncompromising as the exterior. A typical fifteenth-century clerestory allows plenty of light to penetrate the surprisingly spacious nave. Curious niches can be seen in the arcade pillars, which once held figures of Our Lord, Our Lady and five other saints.

England's complex geological structure is the main reason for the wide variety of styles and materials exhibited by the country's churches. Before the Industrial Revolution, transportation of stone was virtually impossible in any quantity, other than by water, and only the rich monasteries could afford such an operation. Church-builders therefore made use of whatever materials were locally available.

Until well into the Middle Ages England was thickly forested so timber was the natural choice for building. The Normans replaced many of these early wooden churches with stone, although the use of wood continued in some areas until the fifteenth century – Hereford and Worcester, and Cheshire retaining the best examples of timber framing. Wood continued to be used for belfries, which were often quite complex in their construction in order to support their considerable load. Essex and Kent still have interesting groups of timber spires and belfries, Blackmore and Brooklands being two of the best.

Oolitic limestone was the most sought after stone, its durability and fine-grained texture making it the ideal medium for church-building. A crescent-shaped band of limestone sweeps down from the North Yorkshire coast to the Channel at Purbeck in Dorset (which is famous for its grey polished limestone 'marble'). This band encompasses Lincolnshire, Leicestershire, the Cotswolds, Wiltshire and Somerset, all of which counties exhibit examples of church masonry at its best.

The 'wool' churches of the Cotswolds are particularly sumptuous. Gradual clearance of the forests provided great sheep runs and men were more than willing to spend their new-found wealth on such lavishly constructed churches as Northleach and Fairford, both in Gloucestershire. Further southwest in Somerset is a remarkable collection of church towers, mostly Perpendicular from the fifteenth century. Some of these achieve heights well in excess of 100 feet, and all are noted for the complexity of their carving and decoration, which would not have been possible with a lesser-quality stone. Even so one wonders how the masons were able to produce such fine tracery and delicate patterning.

Limestone varies in colour and texture, and not all is as durable as the oolitic. Sandstone is the other sedimentary rock most favoured by builders, but in some areas it is very prone to weathering. Parts of Cheshire and the West Midlands have many churches whose walls are pitted and eroded, with exterior carvings blurred and gravestone tributes long since dissolved. The colouring of sandstone also varies, not all being the red or pink shade associated with this rock. West Keal in Lincolnshire is built of New Red sandstone, but its church is a subtle blend of greens, greys and browns.

The country's extreme east and west borders have produced exceptions to the normal pattern of building. Most of East Anglia is devoid of good stone, being on the fringe of the chalk belt that forms the Chilterns and the Downs. A product of the chalk is flint, which unusual material is used on many Norfolk and Suffolk churches. The small irregular-shaped stones were readily gathered from the fields, but the excessive amounts of mortar required when using them for walling often spoilt the effect. Flushwork, where knapped (fractured) flints are used in conjunction with limestone to provide attractive decorations and patterns, is more successful and fine examples can be seen on the spectacular wool churches of Suffolk. Long Melford and Lavenham are two outstanding ones. Round towers, many of them Saxon and Norman, are an East Anglian feature, since it was impossible to make sound corners with flintwork. Thatch is also common due to the lack of stone and abundance of reeds from the Fens.

The majority of Cornwall's churches are built from England's most unyielding stone, granite. The difficulty in working with such a hard and grainy material can be recognized by the absence of carving and other decoration, also by the huge size of many of the stone blocks used in building. Before industry came to the aid of the mason it was common practice to collect the large stones that lay scattered over the surface of the moors and fields. Despite being spared the task of quarrying, dressing the stone must still have been a laborious task.

In most regions there are churches that do not follow the local pattern of building, be it for geological, economic or social reasons, but this merely adds to the pleasure to be gained from exploring the ever-changing architectural landscape of England.

ST MARGARET
HERRINGFLEET, SUFFOLK

Although the village was once on the tidal waters of the River Waveney, its name derives from the Viking family of Herala, who settled here, and not from any romantic or industrial connection with fish.

St Margaret's has a particularly fine example of the East Anglian round tower, dating from the early part of the eleventh century. When first erected the tower was almost certainly free standing and used as a store for weapons and looted valuables, and as a lookout. Some time around 1080, what is now the chancel was built as a small chapel. The nave was not added until the thirteenth century when all three components were linked.

The interior has a set of pews with prominent poppy-head carvings. But perhaps the most exciting features are the east window and the collection of painted glass, brought back from Cologne in Germany by Henry Mussended Leathes. Leathes visited Cologne after participating in Wellington's victory at Waterloo.

ST WINWALLOE
LANDEWEDNACK, CORNWALL

England's most southerly church is one of many in Cornwall to have an unusual dedication. A large number of the Celtic saints came over to England from Ireland or Brittany, but seldom travelled out of the Southwest. Landewednack is situated at the foot of the Lizard peninsula, a location that is geologically unique in this country due to the presence of serpentine stone.

St Winwalloe's is built of granite mixed with this unusual stone, the serpentine being most noticeable in the tower where the large, rough-hewn blocks of dark green, brown and blue-grey rock mix with the granite to give an effect not unlike a crossword puzzle. Add to this a covering of golden lichen, a tree-shaded churchyard and you have one of the most delightful sights to be found anywhere in England.

ST ANDREW
SAMPFORD COURTENAY, DEVON

St Andrew's overlooks a peaceful village of thatched, colour-washed cottages. All was not so serene in 1549 when Sampford Courtenay was at the centre of the Prayer Book Rebellion, a protest against the replacement of the Latin prayer book by a new English version, as decreed by Edward VI. Joined by many other rebels from Devon and Cornwall, the local inhabitants laid siege to Exeter for five weeks but were driven back with dreadful casualties.

The church is from the early sixteenth century, and is built of silvery granite with a graceful, four-pinnacled tower covered in golden lichen. Absence of stained glass gives the interior a wonderful feeling of spaciousness, and the light accentuates the textures on the stone arcading – partly granite and partly grey Polyphant from east Cornwall.

Much rebuilding was done during the nineteenth century, the screen and woodwork suffering as a result, although the screen has since been partially restored. Original carved roof bosses include the arms of the Courtenay family, a king and queen, and symbols of the Holy Trinity.

ST JAMES
KINGSTON, DORSET

Although the central tower of St James's provides a significant landmark, its dominance of the Purbeck countryside will always be secondary to the impressive remains of Corfe Castle, Kingston's closest neighbour. The church was commissioned in 1873 by the third Earl of Eldon, and the architect, Street, always maintained that Kingston was one of his favourite designs. Lord Eldon spent in the region of £70,000 on the construction of this Victorian Gothic masterpiece, which in those days was quite a considerable sum.

The whole building is of locally quarried grey Purbeck limestone, which, in its polished state is transformed into Purbeck marble that is almost black in colour. This contrast is used to great effect in St James's interior, the nave arches resting on dark, shiny columns. The windows too have marble work around them and this black-and-white patterning throughout helps to soften the austere atmosphere that could easily overwhelm an otherwise cold, grey church.

The tower houses a full peal of eight bells, ranging from a treble of $6\frac{3}{4}$ cwt to a tenor weighing $26\frac{3}{4}$ cwt. St James's bells are noted for their quality and the small Parish often reverberates with the efforts of visiting campanologists.

ST MARY THE VIRGIN
BISHOP'S LYDEARD, SOMERSET

Somerset churches are renowned for their Perpendicular towers and interior woodwork, especially rood screens. The church at Bishop's Lydeard, a village at the foot of the Quantock Hills, is no exception. Built of sandstone with Ham Hill limestone dressing, its tower achieves both height and massiveness, appearing to dwarf the rest of the church. The tracery of the belfry becomes more complex with each stage, culminating in pairs of windows at the top whose fine decoration looks almost like lace.

Although the tower is most impressive, it is more than matched for beauty by the screen, which has been perfectly restored to its former glory by Sir Ninian Comper. Its style is common to the West Country, with ornate fan vaulting and delicate carving painted predominantly in red and gold. The Apostles' Creed, written in Latin, runs across the full width of the screen.

St Mary's also possesses a notable collection of Tudor carved bench ends, with finely etched figures and a rare depth of colour not usually found on this kind of work. This colourful interior is further enhanced by an elaborate gold canopy over the altar.

ST MARY THE VIRGIN
FAIRFORD, GLOUCESTERSHIRE

St Mary the Virgin may not be as grand as some of the county's fifteenth-century 'wool' churches, but it is still a perfect example of the Perpendicular style. Embattled parapets with pinnacles run round the entire building and the graceful central tower has twin pinnacles on each corner.

Fairford is famous for its collection of medieval stained glass. Most churches are proud to have retained a few sections over the centuries, but St Mary's has kept it all. A staggering array of light, imagery and colour is spread over the twenty-eight windows, which total about 2,000 square feet of glass. The windows have been removed for safety twice in the church's history, once in the perilous times of Cromwell, and once during the Second World War.

The masterpiece of the collection is the great west window in the nave. Here is the Last Judgement in all its glory and horror. The artist's imagination has known no bounds in his portrayal of Hell, whereas Heaven is a place of light where Jesus is surrounded by the good and innocent.

ST PETER AND ST PAUL
NORTHLEACH, GLOUCESTERSHIRE

Northleach is one of the best Perpendicular Cotswold 'wool' churches, refashioned and enlarged in the fifteenth century by John Farley, a wealthy clothier whose brass is under the north arcade of the nave. The tall clerestory has an exceptionally large nine-light window over the chancel arch, a style similar to others in the region and often referred to as a 'Cotswold' window.

St Peter and St Paul is renowned for its south porch, which is arguably the finest in England. This complex two-storey structure is adorned with pinnacles, statue-filled niches and finely carved panels, and surmounted by an unusual sanctus bellcote. A fireplace in the upper storey indicates that someone once lived there, but who or when is not known.

In 1964 the chancel was turned into a chapel, an altar being established in the nave. This arrangement works very well since the chancel was never able to match the elegance of the nave – possibly because the clergy were responsible for the chancel's upkeep, while the parish looked after the nave.

ST AUGUSTINE
BROOKLAND, KENT

Brookland is typical of the churches on Romney Marsh in that it is totally individual and unspoiled. Dedicated to the first Archbishop of Canterbury, it is perhaps best known for the detached bell tower, a curious wooden arrangement that rather resembles three candle snuffers stacked together. It was originally thought that the belfry was built in the fifteenth century from wrecked ships' timbers, but examination has proved the centre posts to be contemporary with the church, mid thirteenth century. The belfry's shape was made octagonal some time later and the whole structure eventually covered with wooden shingles, currently of cedar.

The church is entered through a medieval porch that has two sets of white painted shutter gates, almost like stable doors, with the top pair shaped to fit the arch. St Augustine's interior is spacious and bright, there being no stained glass. Sadly, the Victorian 'restorers' have left their mark in the chancel, which has been modernized, but the rest has a delightful topsy-turvy feel. This is accentuated by the unequally spaced nave arcades – six on the north side, seven on the south – and by the perilous angle at which the aisle arcades lean.

Brooklands possesses one of the best remaining lead fonts in the country, older than the church, it may have come from France in the twelfth century. Two bands of decoration show in clear detail the signs of the zodiac and the labours of the months.

ST MARY THE VIRGIN
HIGH HALDEN, KENT

Although Essex is generally regarded as the county of timber spires and bell towers, Kent also has some good examples, and none better than at High Halden.

St Mary the Virgin has two exciting pieces of timber construction: its fourteenth-century porch and great belfry. Half tree trunks were used to form the curve of the main arch in the porch and most of the wood is original, some of it showing skilled carving. Boarding and shingles on the bell tower hide an incredible sight, a confusing network of giant, rough-adzed beams that provide bracing and support for the weight of the bells. It is estimated that over 50 tons of oak were used to build the porch and belfry.

Entry to the church is in fact through a lobby beneath the bell tower, lined with Perpendicular panelling. A Norman church existed here and the basic aisleless nave and short chancel have been altered and added to at later periods, much of what we see today dating from the thirteenth and fourteenth centuries.

The Lady Chapel is attractively decorated in blue and silver with natural-coloured oak furniture. One window contains an Annunciation scene of fifteenth-century stained glass.

ST MICHAEL AND ALL ANGELS
GARWAY, HEREFORD AND WORCESTER

The solid square tower of St Michael's resembles a castle keep, a sure indication of a border church and, indeed, Wales is but an arrow's flight across the River Monnow.

Garway belonged to the Knights Templars and the excavated foundations of the original round church are visible. The thirteenth-century detached tower was joined to the nave by a short passage about 300 years ago; the church and tower now sit at a curious angle to each other. The ground floor of the tower is still referred to locally as the 'Prison' so it may have been used for secular purposes over the years.

The original church is represented by a fine Norman chancel arch with three layers of chevron patterning, the capitals having a typical water-leaf design. On the south side of the chancel is the Templars' chapel with an Early English three-arched arcade, partially rebuilt by the Tudors.

Hidden away among the adjoining farm buildings is a circular dovecote, built by the Knights Hospitallers who took over the church after the Templars were disbanded. The walls of the dovecote are 4 feet thick and there is space for 666 birds.

ST BARTHOLOMEW
VOWCHURCH, HEREFORD AND WORCESTER

Vowchurch lies in the middle of Hereford's Golden Valley, so named because of a misinterpretation by the Normans, who translated the Welsh word for water, *dwr*, as *d'or*, the French for gold. However, with its orchards and wheatfields this lovely secluded place still lives up to its name.

St Bartholomew's is fourteenth century and has an attractive half-timbered belfry on top of which is a shingled spirelet. The money for the bell tower was provided by Thomas ApHarry, to whom there is an incised slab in the church, dated 1522, showing him in full armour.

Inside the church there is an unusual system of roof supports, the timbers resting on huge wooden piers set into the walls. This restructuring of the roof was done around 1613. The screen was made at the same period and bears carvings of Adam and Eve and a panel with the following inscription, 'Heare below by the body of Thomas Hill ande Margaret his wife whose children made this skryne.'

ST MARY THE VIRGIN
KETTON, LEICESTERSHIRE

England's smallest county. Rutland, fought long and hard to retain its independence but was finally annexed to Leicestershire in 1974.

This area boasts some of the finest churches in England, perhaps because it also has some of the best building stone. Ketton and Clipsham both have quarries that have been worked for hundreds of years and are still producing grey oolitic limestone. Oddly enough, St Mary's was built of Barnack stone from nearby Northamptonshire.

Broach spires are one of the chief features of the East Midlands and Ketton was much admired by the Victorians as a perfect example. The spire itself is fourteenth century and sits on a beautiful Early English tower whose belfry has sets of graceful round arches on each face.

Transitional architecture is featured on the church's west front, the rest of the building being mainly thirteenth century, although the chancel was largely rebuilt in 1863 by Sir Thomas Jackson. He was able to replace a large, square seventeenth-century window with lancets that were more in keeping with the rest of the church. The panelled roof of the chancel has been painted as it would have appeared in medieval times.

ST PETER
KIRBY BELLARS, LEICESTERSHIRE

A mixture of ironstone and limestone combine to produce a really effective blend of colours and textures, the smooth honey-coloured limestone perfectly complementing the darker brown, more weathered ironstone. An elegant, ornamented broach spire rises above the church to serve as a noticeable landmark.

This is hunting countryside and it was probably here that the word 'steeplechase' originated. In an area blessed with so many spires, the day's sport would be to race between two steeples from village to village in a direct line across country.

St Peter's is partly thirteenth century with enlargements and alterations following later in the Decorated and Perpendicular periods. At one time it became a collegiate church and then later, in 1359, a house of Augustinian Canons.

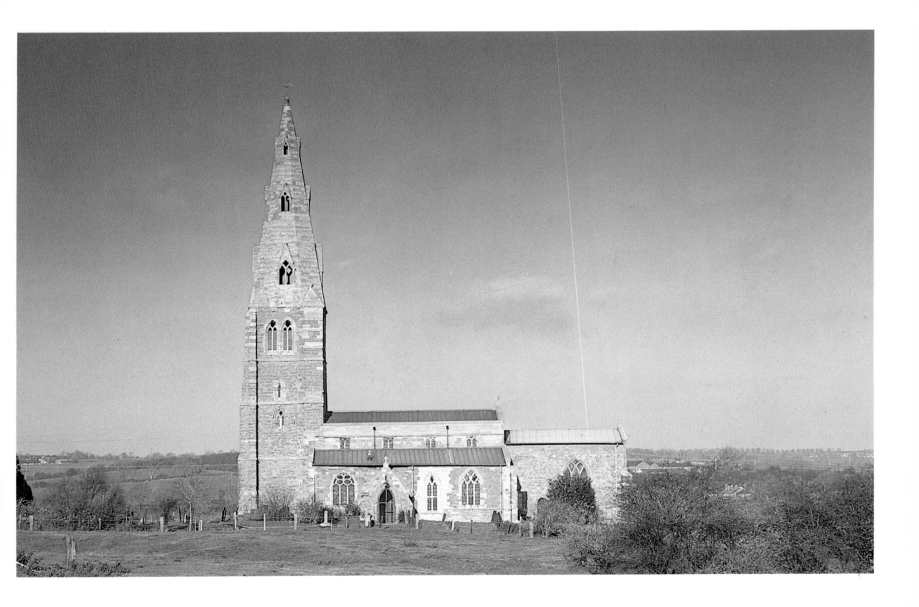

ST MARY THE VIRGIN
WENDENS AMBO, ESSEX

Great and Little Wenden were combined to form one parish in 1662, Ambo merely being the Latin for 'both', hence the current name. St Mary the Virgin lies at the end of a tiny lane lined with typical Essex thatched and tiled cottages, its solid Norman tower being the only part visible through the trees. The tower is topped by a thin shingled spire, more common in the neighbouring county and referred to as a 'Hertfordshire spike'.

Various additions have been made to the original plan, south and north aisles were built in the thirteenth and fourteenth centuries respectively, and a clerestory added to the nave about 1500. Extra windows were put in later, possibly to throw more light on the great rood or crucifix. The rood went the way of all such effigies at the Reformation but most of the screen remains, exhibiting some fine traceried panels.

Modern pews have been cleverly modified to incorporate the medieval bench ends, thereby preserving the atmosphere of the interior. A vivid brass of a man in armour dated to about 1410 is fixed on the south-aisle wall. Sir William Lovenay did not actually die until 1436, but it was common practice then to prepare such memorials in advance.

ST MICHAEL
WOODHAM WALTER, ESSEX

Essex lacks good building stone, so many of the churches in this region are of brick, which has been made and used here since the thirteenth century. Sometimes just the tower, but in many cases the whole church has been constructed of bright red brick, now gently mellowed with age.

Woodham Walter is not as imposing as some churches in the county, but epitomizes the charm and warmth exhibited by these brick buildings. St Michael's is essentially Gothic in style, although built in 1563, and has attractive stepped gables at both ends. The bell turret is a later nineteenth-century addition. The Perpendicular style is represented by the windows, roof and font, which is large and octagonal and decorated with tracery.

The interior colouring of brick churches can be overwhelming, particularly when red tiles have been used for the flooring. Woodham Walter has achieved a harmonious balance and is most pleasing.

ST LEONARD
FLAMSTEAD, HERTFORDSHIRE

Chalk and flint are the two main building materials found in Hertfordshire and as a consequence the churches tend to vary in style and construction. However, one peculiarity exhibited by many is a spirelet known as the 'Hertfordshire spike', a needle-thin spike on top of the tower, usually shingled and then encased in lead. Flamstead's is a typical example.

Large parts of St Leonard's date from the fourteenth century, but the nave is Early English and displays on the capitals the stiff leaf carving that is common to this period.

One of the best medieval wall paintings in Hertfordshire is preserved in the church, showing St Christopher, Christ in Glory and details of the Last Supper. Also discovered this century under layers of plaster was one of the original consecration crosses, which denotes the spot anointed with holy oil during the church's dedication.

HOLY TRINITY
LONG MELFORD, SUFFOLK

The wealth and prosperity of the Suffolk wool and cloth merchants are reflected in the grandeur of this church, built towards the end of the fifteenth century. John Clopton was the main benefactor and there are several brasses to members of his family set into the floor immediately outside their chantry chapel, an intimate room magnificently decorated.

In true Perpendicular style the walls of the church seem to be made of glass, so numerous are the windows. Many of these are clear but there is also a notable collection of medieval coloured glass, particularly in the north aisle.

Near the high altar is the elaborate tomb of Sir William Cordell, Speaker of the House of Commons and Master of the Rolls, who died in 1580. His tomb is the work of Cornelius Cure who was also responsible for monuments to Queen Elizabeth I and Mary Wueen of Scots in Westminster Abbey.

The outside walls of Holy Trinity are covered in an intricate pattern of flushwork – flints carefully split and then inlaid into the stone. Although the tower looks contemporary with the rest of the church it was not built until 1903, a distinct improvement on the brick one it replaced.

ST MARGARET
HALES, NORFOLK

The Norman church of Hales is set on its own away from the village. The community no longer uses the building for worship and it is now in the care of the Redundant Churches Fund.

All three regional characteristics are found in St Margaret's: a thatched roof, a round tower and walls of rough flint. The church dates back to about 1150. It still retains its original rounded apse and few alterations have been made to the windows since the twelfth century.

Some early fifteenth-century wall paintings of St Christopher and St James can be found inside, together with the remains of a screen and an interesting Jacobean font cover.

ST HELEN
WEST KEAL, LINCOLNSHIRE

One of the finest views in Lincolnshire is from St Helen's churchyard, looking across the Fens to 'Boston Stump', the inappropriately named tower of St Botulph's on the edge of the Wash – it is actually 272 feet high.

Local green sandstone provided the main building material for the church, which is a mixture of Perpendicular and Early English styles. Not renowned for its weathering properties, the stone has been patched with brick on some buttresses and corners. The present tower is fairly recent since the original succumbed to high winds one Sunday morning in 1881.

The nave has a north and south aisle, a clerestory with five windows on each side, and arcades of five bays. The capitals on the north side contain dramatic sets of carvings, covering a range of subjects usually found on wooden bench ends. Such detailed work on such a small scale says much for the skill of the masons.

The hues of the local stone are best seen in the porch, parts of which have been recently restored. No two stones are the same shade, greens, greys and browns being subtly blended together.

ST OSWALD
LOWER PEOVER, CHESHIRE

At the end of a long cobbled lane, St Oswald's forms an attractive group of buildings with an inn, the old school and several cottages. The church is an impressive survivor of the timber-framed buildings erected in the Middle Ages. Wood was a plentiful and easily worked material but tended to deteriorate rapidly when in contact with the earth. Oak was the most durable and widely used timber.

Built in 1269 with huge timber frames supported by numerous cross members and braces, the church has obviously undergone restoration but has managed to retain much of its original atmosphere, particularly inside. The sandstone tower was added in 1582, the mellow colour blending well with the black-and-white walls.

Due to the presence of so much wood, the interior is rather dark, but not gloomy, the Jacobean oak furnishings contributing to a richness and warmth that stone churches cannot often give. Many of the box pews still have their original doors with the lower sections fixed to keep the piles of rushes in. Before the advent of flooring or heating, the pews were strewn with rushes to a depth of about a foot during the winter months. Ceremonial rush-bearing services are still held in some parishes in either autumn or spring.

ST JAMES AND ST PAUL
MARTON, CHESHIRE

Much more delicate than its neighbour, Lower Peover, Marton has not been altered or restored with anything but timber since it was founded in 1343. Originally a chantry chapel endowed by Sir John de Davenport, it passed to the Crown at the Dissolution, but the family were able to regain it later. Two worn and eroded effigies of knights in armour, now in the belfry, are thought to be those of Sir John and his son.

The inside of the tower is fascinating for its collection of wooden upright beams and crosspieces, seemingly in a jumble but in fact carefully constructed to distribute the weight and stress of the bells. Three of the original four bells remain, one was removed in 1800. In common with many other timber churches, the belfry was built separately from the nave; some have completely detached bell towers.

Although much restoration has been necessary, Marton still claims to be one of the oldest specimens of wood-and-plaster construction in Europe. With its neatly shingled spirelet and magpie patterning it can certainly boast of being one of the most attractive.

ST MARGARET AND ST JAMES
LONG MARTON, CUMBRIA

Old Red sandstone is the material used for this ancient church, whose village is one of several sheltering under the great bulk of Cross Fell, the highest point of the Pennine hills. The earliest parts of the church date back to about 1100 and there is evidence that suggests this site was a place of worship for centuries before that. Stones have been found with Druid symbols carved into them in addition to other designs of great antiquity.

The tower was added in 1200, which is also when the chancel was lengthened. Most of the windows were enlarged during the fifteenth century, replacing the original ones, which were too high up and too small to provide any kind of efficient lighting.

The tympana over the original south and west doors show pictorial carvings with traces of Saxon influence; a dragon and winged ox in a boat, dragons and mermen, all typical of the imagery found in many Romanesque churches.

By the late nineteenth century the building was in urgent need of repair, and was virtually gutted and rebuilt. Most of the work was carried out sympathetically, particularly the new hammer-beam roof of Hereford oak.

ST MICHAEL
BURGH-BY-SANDS, CUMBRIA

Hadrian's Wall became one of the best stone quarries in the north of England, many churches and large houses benefiting from the work of the Roman masons. St Michael's is a solidly fortified border church on the edge of the Solway Firth, a few miles to the west of Carlisle.

It dates mainly from the late Norman and Early English periods. Close inspection of the stonework will reveal traces of Roman carving on blocks that have been taken from the Wall in addition to marks made by the sharpening of weapons in readiness for repelling raiders.

A little way to the north of the church on the estuary marshes is a large monument to Edward I who spent a good deal of time trying to contain the Scottish threat. He died in camp during one such campaign in 1307.

ST ANNE
ANCROFT, NORTHUMBERLAND

A short distance from the Northumbrian coast, Ancroft was one of four chapelries established by the monks of Holy Island. The stone for the priory on Lindisfarne came from the parish of Ancroft so the church was built as an offering of thanks. Several sections of the original building remain, and are thought to date back to 1089. The tower is early fourteenth century and a rare example of a fortified 'vicar's pele' that is actually joined on to the church. These towers were usually the residences of clergymen, doubling as hideouts in times of trouble. There is a fireplace in the upper storey, but it still represents spartan living.

By the mid nineteenth century the building was fairly dilapidated, and restoration has resulted in a lot of Victorian glass and furniture. Fortunately the exterior has retained its solid, somewhat austere look, very much in keeping with the north-country landscape.

HOLY TRINITY
CHAPEL STILE, GREAT LANGDALE, CUMBRIA

The old chapel from which the village derives its name was replaced by the present church in 1858. The population had increased rapidly in the nineteenth century with the opening of a gunpowder works to supply the needs of the local quarries that were producing the area's much sought after green slate.

Holy Trinity is built of this material and seems to be so well camouflaged against the rock face that at times it is almost invisible. The slate came from the nearby quarry on Silver How and during the building work planks were laid from the fellside to the top of the tower to make its transfer easier.

Slate is an attractive stone, but can never be as impressive as the limestones or granite for church-building. This is largely due to the way it fractures into wedge-shaped pieces, which makes the use of large quantities of cement inevitable. Viewed from a distance this is not really noticeable, but when seen close up the subtle colours of the slate are broken up by great zigzags of cement filling.

ESTATE AND ABBEY CHURCHES

ALL SAINTS
GREAT CHALFIELD, WILTSHIRE

The manor house and church of Great Chalford are a pleasing sight. The house, which could be from the Cotswolds with its warm yellow stone, gables and mullioned windows, was built in 1470 by Thomas Tropenell, a successful politician and landowner, and traces of the original moat are still evident although now much overgrown and clogged with weeds and rushes.

Tropenell refashioned the thirteenth-century church and added the rather quaint spire and bellcote, as well as building his own family chapel. This is entered from the nave through a Perpendicular stone screen emblazoned with heraldry. Sections of mutilated wall paintings enable one to imagine how grand and colourful the chapel must have been when in use, and there are six painted panels, in better condition, depicting the life of St Catherine.

The National Trust rescued and restored the house in 1943 after many years of neglect.

Estate and abbey churches have been grouped together because they often have one thing in common: decline over the years may have reduced their stature, but their elegance and location provide vivid impressions of former grandeur.

Some of our finest parish churches were originally monastic buildings until Henry VIII's Dissolution of the Monasteries in the 1530s. Occasionally the whole church has survived – Sherborne, Edington and Cartmel being notable examples – but more usually only that part of the church that was used for parochial worship was spared. In most cases the stripping of lead from the roof led to rapid decay, many buildings simply crumbling into ruin around the portion used for the parish church. After the Conquest, William granted a quarter of all land in England to the Church, and this wealth was manifest in the opulence of monastic churches. Although added to over the centuries, many abbeys still retain the influence of the Norman architects, who seemed able to create a great feeling of space even within a relatively contained area.

The majority of abbeys and priories belonged to one of three distinct orders: Benedictine, Augustinian and Cistercian. St Benedict founded his order in Monte Cassino, Italy, early in the sixth century, and his doctrine reached England about AD 950. The Benedictines were known as the 'Black Monks' (from their black habits), and the order followed a rule of obedience, poverty, regular prayer, manual work and scholarship. The Benedictines were the strongest of the Norman religious orders, Augustinians forming the next largest group. The Augustinian Canons were not monks but ordained priests living monastic lives according to the writings of St Augustine (AD 345–430), the order being introduced to England around 1100. Cistercians were referred to as the 'White Monks' (again from the colour of their clothes) and, although their order was the most strict of the three, many of their monasteries displayed some of the finest architecture to be found anywhere in the country. Sadly, most of the great Cistercian houses are now famous ruins; Fountains Abbey and Riveaulx in Yorkshire are two that provide glimpses of an impressive past. Abbey Dore in Hereford is one parish church that retains some of the atmosphere and scale of a great monastic church, despite being reduced to transepts and chancel.

The origins of estate churches go back to Saxon and Norman times when the thane or lord would have built a church for himself and his household; the village or parish church as we know it followed later. Although many of the present estate churches have Norman or medieval histories, it was the seventeenth and eighteenth centuries that produced the best examples of an often unashamedly indulgent architecture. The great landowners of the eighteenth century would frequently erect a church to adorn their newly landscaped parkland, even going to the extent of demolishing the existing building regardless of its condition. Such an operation was nothing to men who resited whole villages because they happened to be too close to the manor house; the tenants often acquired better housing but had a longer trek to church on a Sunday morning.

Quite a large number of estate churches were influenced by the design of other buildings. Continental styles reflect memories of travels abroad. Domes and pillars are prevalent, influences from Tuscany and Greece – no expense was spared to cater to the whims of the owners. Some designs are quite hideous and bear no resemblance to traditional church architecture, but other buildings, like Well, in Lincolnshire, were based on the work of well-known architects, in this case Inigo Jones's St Paul's in Covent Garden.

It would be unfair to say that most estate churches lack taste in design, there are many graceful and elegant buildings that perfectly complement the large house or hall to which they belong. Often the family are remembered by a number of monuments varying in size and artistic merit. Some of the older churches are packed so full of marble and alabaster tablets and effigies that there seems to be little room left for the congregation.

The sadness of these churches is that many are now alone, the house having long since collapsed. Only the work of the Redundant Churches Fund prevents the rot and decay that would ultimately result in the loss of these valuable and irreplaceable buildings.

ST MARY AND ST MICHAEL
CARTMEL, CUMBRIA

Cartmel is an unusual example of a former priory turned to parish use in that the whole church survived the Dissolution. This was partly due to the founder, William Marshall, decreeing that an altar and priest be provided for the people. So although the church had been stripped of all metal, including most of the lead from the roof, the south aisle of the choir was still used as a place of worship.

For eighty years this one small portion of the priory church continued in use, while the rest became gradually more ruinous. Eventually, in 1618, George Preston of nearby Holker Hall started a restoration programme, and followed this with the gift of the magnificent screen that now extends around the choir.

The building itself was started in 1190 during the Transitional period. It consists of varying materials: limestone and slate rubble walls, red sandstone and millstone grit for the piers, and Caen stone for the outstanding Perpendicular east window. One unusual external feature is the tower, the top section of which is set diagonally on the base – a unique arrangement.

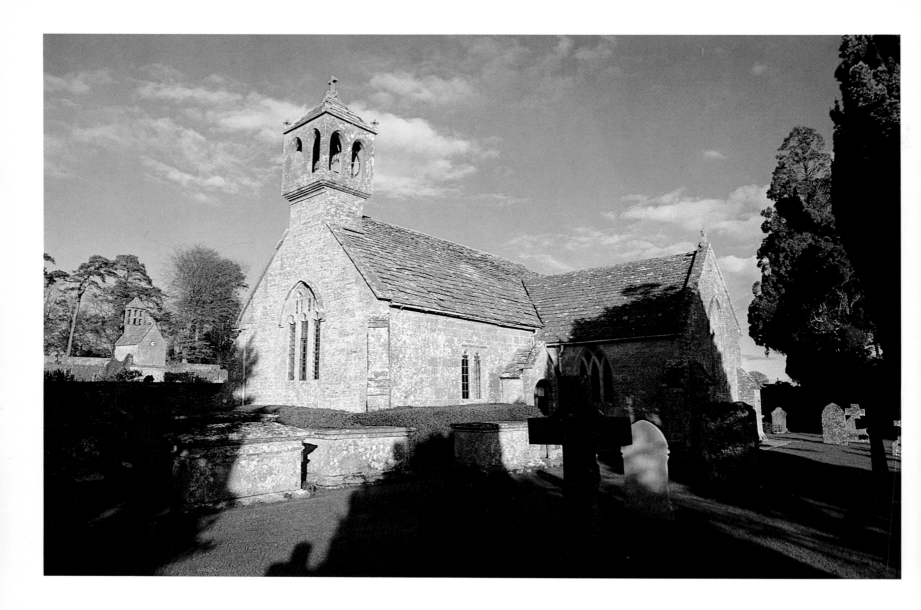

ST ANDREW
BRYMPTON D'EVERCY, SOMERSET

Brympton D'Evercy must be one of the best and most attractive examples of a medieval church that is closely associated with a manor house. The buildings are of the same mellow golden Ham Hill stone and are set in perfect grounds surrounded by low stone walls. As in many cases where a church is attached to a manor, St Andrew's is also the parish church and can be reached by a public right of way from the village.

The church belongs largely to the fourteenth and fifteenth centuries and has a quaint, lantern-like bell turret. Inside, some of the best features include a very good early Perpendicular screen, a fourteenth-century font, eighteenth-century Dutch brass chandeliers, and some interesting effigies – John D'Evercy who wears chain mail and, in a horned headdress, Dame Isobel D'Evercy, widow of John's successor, Peter.

In addition to the family memorials there is a monument to a priest, shown holding a chalice. This is a tribute to the parish priest who, according to legend, died while administering last rites during the Black Death in 1349. On the wall above the priest is a relief of the Nativity that shows an early attempt at perspective – one cow being placed directly above another.

ST LAWRENCE
FOLKE, DORSET

The attractive church of St Lawrence sits next to the manor house in a tranquil corner of Blackwater Vale. The manor dates back to around 1500, and is one of three historically and architecturally interesting houses in the vicinity.

St Lawrence was rebuilt in its present form in 1628 and is furnished in Jacobean style. The screens with their interlaced bands of decoration and the pulpit with reeded panels are particularly fine, and there is an hour-glass stand next to the pulpit.

The tower and all the external walls are embattled in Gothic fashion. An unusual feature are the attractive triplet windows, which have very tall centre lights.

ST MARY THE VIRGIN
SHERBORNE, DORSET

The honey-golden abbey of local Ham Hill stone seems to dwarf the centre of this peaceful market town. Sherborne's well-documented history goes back to AD 705 and its first bishop, St Aldhelm. Discoveries over the years have led experts to believe that the original Saxon cathedral was almost as big as the present church. Some pre-Conquest and Norman features remain incorporated in today's building, but the overall style is essentially Perpendicular.

Undoubtedly the greatest feature of St Mary's is the fan vaulting over nave and choir, some of the earliest and finest in the country. The whole of the choir is exquisitely coloured and presents a truly magnificent example of soaring Perpendicular architecture at its best. Fifteenth-century misericords show extraordinary carved details, including a boy being birched and a woman beating a man.

The Early English period of the thirteenth century is perfectly represented by the Lady Chapel, which is entered through an elegant arch supported by shafts of Purbeck marble.

The bells of St Mary the Virgin are the heaviest peal of eight in the world, with an average weight of just under one ton. The tenor bell, a gift from Cardinal Wolsey, weighs a massive 46 cwt.

ST MARY
WESTWOOD, WILTSHIRE

Westwood manor house – owned by the National Trust – and St Mary's church are located in a quiet part of Wiltshire, close to the Somerset border. The chancel is the oldest part of the church building, being mainly thirteenth century, but possibly having an earlier history since traces of a carved tympanum – evidence of Norman architecture – remain over the priest's doorway.

Some excellent medieval stained glass can be found in the chancel, portraying Christ Crucified surrounded by angels; a total of some twenty figures. Mouldings run round the chancel arch that leads into the nave, which has an elegant plaster ceiling that was put in during eighteenth-century refashioning. This contrasts well with the old timbers and rich panelling of the chancel.

St Mary's is entered through the fifteenth-century tower, built by one of the manor's owners, a wealthy clothier named Thomas Horton, who died in 1530. The Perpendicular tower, which seems to dwarf the church, has finely traceried windows, gargoyles and a highly decorated parapet at one corner of which is a domed turret – a feature that is reflected in the church's interior, the font cover being a perfect copy of the dome.

ST MARY AND ST BLAISE
BOXGROVE, WEST SUSSEX

Boxgrove is an elegant and stately relic of a Benedictine priory, with only the choir, tower and transepts surviving.

The community was founded by monks from Lessay in France, who started work on the priory and church around 1115. Tower and transepts are Norman; the choir, with its vaulted roof, is Early English from the thirteenth century. Considerable use has been made of Purbeck marble, whose dark grey colour contrasts sharply with the pale Caen stone that is employed throughout.

In the sixteenth century, the beautiful vaulting in the choir was further enhanced by painted decoration. The artist was Lambert Barnard, who painted the arms and crests of the de la Warr family entwined with botanical patterns in a Flemish Renaissance style.

In addition to commissioning the decorations to the vaulting, Lord Thomas de la Warr built himself a chantry chapel, most elaborately carved, decorated and coloured. Unfortunately the Dissolution arrived before his death, forcing him to buy the priory in order to save his chantry. It was all to no avail. Chantries were banned and poor Sir Thomas was buried elsewhere.

THE BLESSED VIRGIN MARY, ST KATHERINE AND ALL SAINTS
EDINGTON, WILTSHIRE

This imposing, battlemented church stands immediately below the steep escarpment of Salisbury plain, with breathtaking views rolling far away to the north. It is a surprise to find such an impressive building next to a tiny Wiltshire village and well away from any sizeable community.

The grey, cruciform church was built by William of Edington, Bishop of Winchester and treasurer to Edward III. His intention had been to establish a chantry for himself and his family at his birthplace, but after some persuasion from the Black Prince he enlarged the plans and founded an Augustinian monastery instead; the church was finally consecrated in 1361.

Edington is of some architectural importance as it marks the transition from Decorated to Perpendicular styles. This pattern can be followed throughout the building, the windows providing the most noticeable change of direction.

Nave and chancel are separated by a great oak screen, dated to about 1500. Before the Dissolution, the nave was used for worship by the parishioners, the chancel by the monks.

Plaster ceilings from the seventeenth and eighteenth centuries have replaced the original open timber roof, the pink-and-white plaster in the nave somehow working well with the rest of the interior.

ST MARY THE VIRGIN
GLYNDE, EAST SUSSEX

The small village of Glynde on the South Downs has two large period houses of note. Glyndebourne, to the north, is world famous for its opera house. Glynde Place, an Elizabethan mansion, was owned by Richard Trevor, Bishop of Durham, and it was he who built the adjoining church, in 1763–5, to a Palladian design by Sir Thomas Robinson.

The dignified elegance of the Georgian period is reflected here, although the interior has seen the hand of the Victorian restorers. A large walnut screen was erected in 1895, and an incongruous light fitting installed in the nave. All the walls are hung with gold-and-brown patterned hessian giving the impression of a drawing room rather than a church, particularly since the screen has now been removed.

Flemish-style glass by William Kemp contributes to the mellow but sombre feeling inside this unusual building.

ST PETER AND ST PAUL
DORCHESTER, OXFORDSHIRE

Situated almost on the banks of the River Thame and set among willow trees, Dorchester Abbey occupies the site of a seventh-century Saxon cathedral.

Dorchester was an important Roman town that, with the coming of the Saxons in the fifth century, became the centre of a huge diocese. In 1170 the Normans founded an Augustinian abbey here, which remained until the Dissolution in 1536. Fortunately the whole church survived so, apart from a few later additions and some nineteenth-century restoration, we are left with a magnificent building that is mostly of the Decorated period.

Without doubt Dorchester's greatest glory is the fourteenth-century north window in the choir, the 'Jesse' window. This is an intricate blend of sculpture and stained glass, the tracery forming the branches of Christ's family tree, which sprouts from the loins of Jesse, carved in stone beneath the glass. The whole window is full of glazed and sculptured figures depicting the ancestors of Jesus, the angel Gabriel and the three Wise Men.

Another superb piece of art is the thirteenth-century effigy of a knight, frozen in the act of drawing his sword, perhaps in defiance of death.

ST MARY MAGDALENE
CROOME D'ABITOT, HEREFORD AND WORCESTER

Croome Court, once the home of the Earls of Coventry, is now a school. The church stands on a hill overlooking the mansion, both buildings being the work of Capability Brown and Robert Adam. The present church was built in 1763 and replaced an earlier one that was sited a few hundred yards to the west, monuments from which are now in the chancel of St Mary Magdalene.

These huge marble effigies seem rather out of place in the graceful eighteenth-century interior but even so make a formidable collection. The earliest is to Thomas, the first Lord Coventry, who died in 1639, and who is shown in a semi-reclining position. There are separate memorials to the second Lord Coventry and his wife; she is holding a baby indicating that she died in childbirth. Grinling Gibbons executed the carving on the fourth Lord Coventry's monument. Tablets and plaques to later members of the family are distributed round the nave.

St Mary Magdalene's exterior is beautifully proportioned and considered to be an important example of early Gothic Revival. Brown's church was given a very dignified interior by Robert Adam, who was also responsible for such details as the elaborately carved wooden font.

ST MARY
ABBEY DORE, HEREFORD AND WORCESTER

The Golden Valley runs parallel with the nearby Welsh border just east of the Black Mountains. At the southern end of this peaceful haven lies the dark red sandstone church of Abbey Dore.

St Mary's is part of an old Cistercian monastery, now consisting of chancel and transepts. When viewed from a distance the exterior may seem slightly unbalanced. This is due largely to the tower, which was added in the seventeenth century by Viscount Scudamore.

The sheer beauty and elegance of the Early English interior is quite awe inspiring, an effect created by the vast height and space of the transepts and crossing. Here all is light and colour, with many gently faded wall paintings including the royal arms of Queen Anne. Viscount Scudamore commissioned John Abel to design the oak screen, the same architect being responsible for the roof restoration in which 204 tons of local oak were used.

Throughout the church are perfect pointed arches, clusters of subtly decorated columns, and beautifully stained lancet windows, all combining to provide a superb example of the Early English style at its best.

HOLY CROSS
PERSHORE, HEREFORD AND
WORCESTER

Holy Cross is the abbey church of a
Benedictine monastery, which although sadly
mutilated retains much of its former grandeur.
Originally founded about AD 689, Norman
work probably began around AD 1090, and
additional building went on into the
fourteenth century. The parts that remain are
the tower, transepts, chancel and apse, the
original building having been about 325 feet
long. After the Dissolution, the nave and Lady
Chapel were pulled down, and the crossing
tower, which is an impressive piece of early-
fourteenth-century work, was shored up on its
north side in 1686.

The beautiful thirteenth-century vaulting in
the presbytery is worthy of mention, not least
because it is so seldom found in parish
churches, really fine examples usually being
restricted to the grander abbeys and
cathedrals.

All traces of the monastery buildings have
now vanished leaving the mellow limestone
abbey to stand alone.

ST MARY THE VIRGIN
INGESTRE, STAFFORDSHIRE

St Mary the Virgin stands next to the hall
amid grounds once landscaped by Capability
Brown. The Chetwynd family were associated
with Ingestre for many generations, and it
was Walter Chetwynd who built the church in
1673 to a design by Sir Christopher Wren.
This is one of only a few churches by Wren to
be found outside London, and is a most
elegant example of a country church from the
late Stuart period.

In keeping with many churches from this
time the exterior is relatively simple and
square, but the interior is in complete
contrast. The most arresting feature in a
building full of interest must be the ceiling,
which is covered with elaborately decorated
plasterwork. This is typical of a Wren church,
but unfortunately many such examples were
damaged or destroyed during the Second
World War.

Decoration is not reserved solely for the
roof, a three-arched screen and heavy pulpit
with tester are also ornately carved. Both
these pieces have been attributed to Grinling
Gibbons.

The lighting is unusual in that it was
installed in 1886, only three years after the
first London church received electricity. The
tall, wrought-iron fittings blend harmoniously
with their earlier surroundings.

ST CATHERINE
BIRTLES, CHESHIRE

In a county where the churches are mainly of sandstone or millstone or half timbered, the brick-built oddity at Birtles comes as something of a surprise. Even more strange is the octagonal tower, which gives the building a lopsided look. St Catherine's was built in 1840 by the owners of Birtles Hall, a two-storey mansion that burnt down in 1938 and was then completely rebuilt.

The church consists of a nave and short chancel. Most of the furnishings and glass were imported by one of the hall's owners, Thomas Hibbert, the wood having come largely from the Netherlands as is particularly evident in the screen and family pew. Carved figures and old stall backs have been used for the screen; the pew is made up of a mixture of different pieces.

Most of the stained glass is also Continental in origin, much of it from the sixteenth and seventeenth centuries although the main group of figures in the east window, the Virgin, an angel and St John, are thought to be much earlier.

Frescoes on the walls and the candelabra are direct copies from other famous churches. Although there is a rather self-indulgent feel to St Catherine's, it is still a likeable and interesting church.

ST MARY
NETHER ALDERLEY, CHESHIRE

The mansion that was the seat of the Stanley family is no more, but the family's influence lives on in the church, mausoleum and old school, which are all tightly grouped together and built of locally quarried sandstone.

St Mary's dates from the fourteenth century, with a stately tower from a later period. St Lawrence was the original patron saint but there is no recorded evidence as to why the dedication was changed.

A Jacobean addition to the church was the extraordinary family pew, a two-storey affair directly facing and overshadowing the pulpit, rather like an opera box. There is no access from inside the building; entry is gained via a flight of steps and private entrance on the outside wall. The interior of the pew has a coved and decorated ceiling, and an abundance of wood panelling heavily adorned with coats of arms.

St Mary's possesses two old Bibles, one is a 'Vinegar' edition from 1717, the other a 'Breeches' Bible from around 1560.

ST MARY MAGDALENE
STAPLEFORD, LEICESTERSHIRE

Stapleford Hall, formerly the home of the Earls of Harborough, the Sherard family, is a beautiful stone mansion with a Tudor wing that has high gables and mullioned windows. The church, which was rebuilt in 1783 in Gothic style, lies a little way from the house, surrounded by elms, oaks and beeches.

Inside the church are forty shields depicting the arms of the Sherards and the families into which they married. The seating faces inwards as in a college chapel and all the original woodwork remains, including the family pew in the west gallery with its fine Adam fireplace.

There are two monuments from the original church, the oldest being a fifteenth-century brass to Geoffrey Sherard, who is shown in armour with his feet resting on a greyhound and accompanied by his wife and seven children. The other is a seventeenth-century altar tomb in marble to Sir William Sherard. His wife, Lady Abigail, lies beside him and they are surrounded by their eight kneeling children, three of whom are in swaddling cloths.

There are many more monuments and memorials to the Earls of Harborough, covering many generations. The Sherard dynasty ended with the death of the last Earl in 1895.

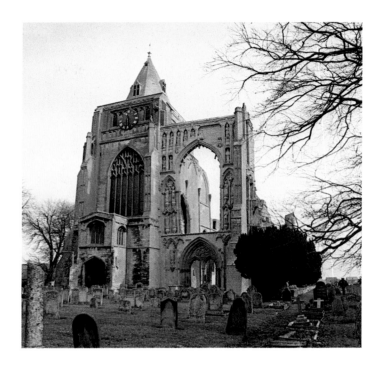

ST MARY WITH ST GUTHLAC AND ST BARTHOLOMEW
CROWLAND, LINCOLNSHIRE

Over 1,200 years ago the Fens were not the well-drained areas of rich farmland that exist today and Crowland was an island in the middle of vast swamps. It was here that St Guthlac came to live as a hermit until his death in 714. Ethelbald, King of Mercia, established the first Benedictine monastery in the saint's memory two years later.

Some of the ruins still standing today are from the third abbey, which was built early in the twelfth century, notably the high, dogtooth moulded arch of the ruined nave. Most dramatic of all is the west front with its rows of statue-filled niches portraying saints, apostles and past abbots of Croyland.

The village is called Crowland, but the abbey has always been Croyland, although there is no evidence to establish when the change happened, or why. The parish church was formed from the abbey's north aisle and dates mainly from the early fifteenth century. It has an impressive stone vaulted roof and a particularly beautiful chancel screen that still retains traces of medieval colouring and gilding. Set into one of the tower arches is what looks like a huge holy water stoup, but is actually a Norman immersion font that holds 25 gallons.

ST MARGARET
WELL, LINCOLNSHIRE

St Margaret's church is a miniature replica of St Paul's, Covent Garden, which was designed by Inigo Jones a hundred years before Well was built. This delightful little Georgian building with its four Tuscan columns is perfectly sited on a hill, looking down over the landscaped parkland and lake towards the house of Well Vale. Great landowners frequently made their churches part of the scenery, a focal point in the view. Very often, as in Well's case, this necessitated demolishing the existing building, which, although perfectly sound, happened to be in the wrong place.

The interior is unspoiled and retains its Georgian atmosphere. A large three-decker pulpit with tester towers over the collegiate-style pews. An ornate stucco ceiling, a royal coat of arms, and a font made from a wooden baluster complete this intimate but strangely imposing place of worship.

Access to the church is by footpath only, a pleasant walk on a sunny morning but an arduous trek in winter for the villagers and estate workers.

HOLY TRINITY
LITTLE OUSEBURN, NORTH YORKSHIRE

Holy Trinity now stands alone, surrounded by what was once the landscaped parkland of Kirby Hall, home of the Thomson family. A domed mausoleum in the churchyard gives an indication of the church's more affluent past; it was built by Henry Thomson in the late eighteenth century and is surrounded by thirteen Tuscan columns. Mausolus, King of Caria, who died in the fourth century BC, gave his name to these magnificent tombs. His own was erected by Queen Artemisia, acting on his instructions.

The church has a tall unbuttressed Norman tower crowned with Perpendicular battlements and pinnacles. The same style is employed in the nave and aisles and two-bay arcade. Two Norman windows remain in the chancel, which also has thirteenth-century lancets and, best of all, a five-light Perpendicular window with intersected tracery.

ALL SAINTS
HOVINGHAM, NORTH YORKSHIRE

Hovingham Hall is the ancestral home of the Worsleys, the Duchess of Kent's family. Sir Thomas designed the hall in the mid eighteenth century, but All Saints', which stands close by, boasts a history far older than its surroundings. The tower is pre-Conquest with typical Saxon features, while the church itself possesses several relics of even greater age. Set into the stones above the door is a carved cross identical in design to St Cuthbert's pectoral cross (four equal arms with flaring ends), which could date it to the eighth century. Cuthbert was bishop of Lindisfarne and died in AD 687.

Also preserved by the Saxon builders is a 'wheel' cross high over the belfry opening. This ancient Christian symbol has a strong Viking influence.

Acting as a reredos in the Lady Chapel is Hovingham's great treasure, a unique Saxon sculptured stone of eight figures. A date of about AD 800 has been attributed to the stone, which was found, built into the tower, in 1924. The Saxon masons had made an attempt, obviously successful, to hide and preserve the ancient carving.

As may be expected, there are a number of monuments to the Worsley family; the church itself is one, dedicated to Marcus Worsley's wife, who died two years before the Victorian 'restoration' that virtually rebuilt the church leaving only the tower unscathed.

ALL SAINTS
SETTRINGTON, NORTH YORKSHIRE

According to a survey of Settrington carried out in 1599, it would seem that the outline of the village has changed little over the years – estate communities are rarely subject to outside influences and development – although the stone cottages were rebuilt in 1800, and the original house was pulled down and a new one erected on the opposite side of the church.

The church itself dates from the twelfth century, but has been refashioned, altered and restored over the years so that no one period of architecture has dominance. Some of the windows, notably in the south aisle, have quantities of original fourteenth- and fifteenth-century glass.

Monuments in the chancel include a brass to John Carter, a rector who, with his wife and children, was forcibly ejected at the time of the Commonwealth. He was reinstated sixteen years later. Lord of the manor Henry Masterman is also remembered in elaborate style.

Heraldry in the church belongs to the Bigod family, who were associated with Settrington between the thirteenth and sixteenth centuries. Their tenure came to an end when Sir Francis was executed for his part in the Pilgrimage of Grace in 1537.

ST MARY
OLD MALTON, NORTH YORKSHIRE

Judging by what remains of this Gilbertine priory, the original must have been quite monumental. The monastic buildings have mostly disappeared leaving only part of the church as a reminder of former glories. The west front with its one remaining tower has a large, late Norman doorway, a huge perpendicular window and masses of arcading.

St Gilbert founded his exclusively English order around 1131, and, of the original twenty-six houses, St Mary's is the only church still in use. The priory here was founded about 1147 by Eustace Fitz-John, the work being completed around 1200. It was not until 1732 that the church we see today was made secure by restoration and rebuilding, decay and dereliction having followed the Dissolution. The nave was shortened and the roof lowered, which resulted in the blocking of the upper part of the great window on the west front.

In the churchyard are some interesting Gothic gravestones, and on the north wall can be found the parish coffin shelf. It used to be common practice to be buried in just a shroud, the communal coffin being merely for transport to the churchyard. This was its resting place between 'jobs'.

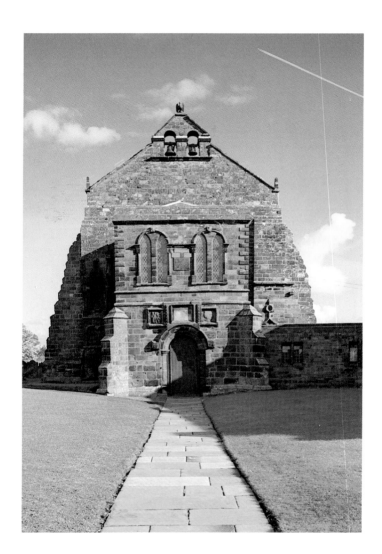

ST MARY
ABBEY TOWN, CUMBRIA

Holm Cultram Abbey was founded in 1150 by Cistercian monks from Melrose Abbey. The Solway region was a part of Scotland in those days, reverting to England in 1157. Throughout its history the abbey suffered greatly from the hazards associated with its location, close to the Solway Firth and the Scottish border, the worst damage being inflicted by Robert the Bruce in 1319, despite the fact that his father was buried at the abbey.

After the Dissolution the local people were successful in their attempts to retain the abbey church as their place of worship, and as a necessary stronghold against the Scots. Even so, the inevitable decay followed, and chancel and transepts were destroyed by the collapse of the tower. Many stones from the buildings ended up in the walls of local barns and cow byres.

A major restoration of the remaining part began in 1703; the nave was reduced to six bays, the aisles removed and the roof lowered. The church is entered through a fine porch, built in 1507 by Abbot Chambers whose monument is immediately inside. Beyond the porch is a superb Norman portal leading into the nave, which although reduced in size retains much of its former grandeur.

ST MARY MAGDALENE
LANERCOST, CUMBRIA

Robert de Vaux founded this house of Augustinian Canons around 1166, and, with the aid of generous endowments, building began on a large scale. Completed by about 1220, it is surprising to discover that, despite its size and the extensive range of buildings, there were usually no more than fifteen canons at the priory at any one time.

Close proximity to the Scottish border meant that time here could not always be devoted entirely to prayer and meditation. Edward I and his entourage used Lanercost as a military base on three occasions. The Scots, on the other hand, merely ransacked the place and then moved on.

The rebuilding necessitated by the Scottish invasions plunged the community into debt leaving it unable to meet the financial conditions laid down by Henry VIII at the Dissolution. The buildings at Lanercost were granted to Sir Thomas Dacre, who converted some of the monastery into a private dwelling. The north aisle was used as the parish church until 1740 when the nave was restored, and it is these two surviving areas that form the church that exists today.

One curious aspect of Lanercost is the extent of the ruined sections. Tower, transepts and choir, all roofless, still stand to their full height.

ST ANDREW
KIRKANDREWS-UPON-ESK, CUMBRIA

Kirkandrews is only a few hundred yards from the western end of the Scottish border, just south of the defensive line called Scotsdyke – evidence of the border's close proximity being provided by the fortified tower that stands in a field close to the church.

Netherby Hall, for which St Andrew's is the estate church, is located on the other side of the Esk river, house and church being linked by a narrow pedestrian suspension bridge. The Hall was made famous by Sir Walter Scott in his novel *Marmion*, in which the Graham family heiress eloped with young Lochinvar.

St Andrew's was rebuilt in 1776 of local red sandstone in a style that seems rather out of keeping with its surroundings; the tower is crowned by an open circle of columns topped with a stone cap, and beneath the tower is a Tuscan doorway.

Temple Moore restored the interior in 1893, the work including the formation of the chancel, and installation of a new organ and an Italian-style green and gold screen.

St Andrew's is not the prettiest of churches, but perhaps its attraction lies in the fact that it does not blend with the surrounding architecture and landscape.

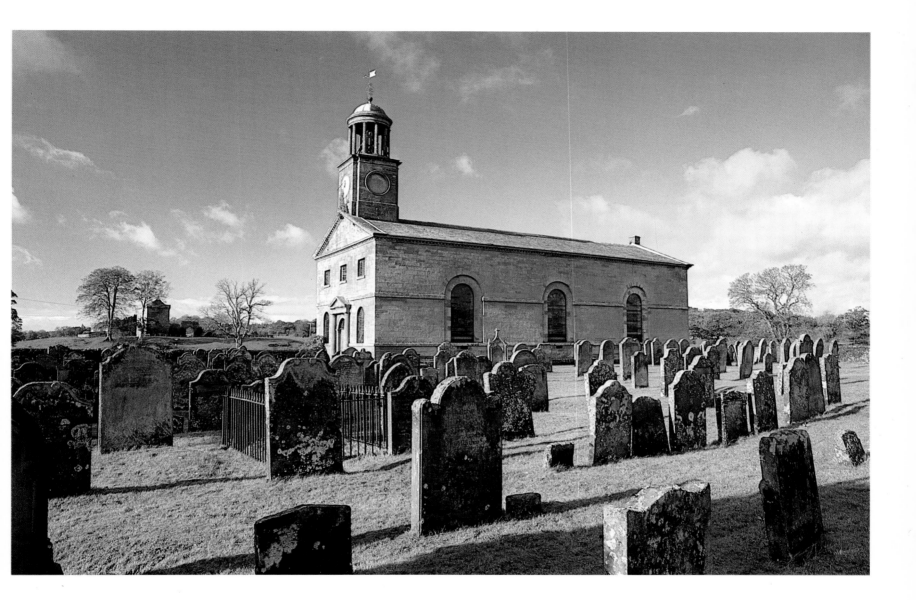

TINY OR ISOLATED CHURCHES

ST THOMAS À BECKET
FAIRFIELD, KENT

It is hard to find a reason for the existence of Fairfield church, whose only parishioners seem to be the sheep, cattle and sea birds that inhabit Romney Marsh, St Thomas's is surrounded by flat lands crisscrossed with ditches, the way to the church being along raised causeways.

There is a startling contrast between the red and blue brick exterior and the timbered interior, which goes back to the fourteenth century. Rebuilding took place in 1913 but the interior was left untouched and unspoiled. Particularly impressive are the huge timber arches that span the chancel, also the tie beams, which are less than 7 feet from the ground.

The fittings are entirely in harmony with the wooden framework and include box pews, text boards and a three-decker pulpit. An interesting set of old photographs is hung near the font showing the various stages of the reconstruction work.

Isolated churches seemingly far away from habitation are not always the smallest, although it often happens that both descriptions are applicable. For instance, where the purpose of a church was to enable a small, scattered community to worship without having to make a long journey to a distant parish church in the nearest village or town, then it would have been pointless to erect a building to accommodate large numbers. Many of these small chapels were in fact not licensed for marriages or burials – that remained the right of the Mother church – but all had a font. In the days of high infant mortality this facility was essential to ensure that no child died without baptism. Some of these remoter churches in wild moorland settings can be difficult to locate, detailed maps and a good deal of patience and perseverance often being required to find them.

There are fascinating larger churches too that have become stranded for a variety of reasons. In the case of some estate churches it is because the place of worship has survived long after the disappearance of the house and community it was meant to serve. Other religious sites have a history that goes back far beyond the birth of Christianity, having been used through the centuries as holy places irrespective of the gods being worshipped there. This continuity has often led to a church being set well away from its community.

Although the majority of isolated churches still offer clues as to the reason for their location, there are a number that defy all logic. Who could fail to wonder at the position of Brentor church in the middle of Dartmoor? Perched on top of an ancient volcanic cone 1,100 feet above sea level, it could serve equally well as a fortress, the only access being by a steep, often muddy path that would deter the most hostile invaders.

The development of larger, more mechanized farms and the gradual drift of the population to the cities with their higher-paid industries contributed to the desertion of the countryside. In recent years this trend has been reversed and more people are trying to 'get away from it all', back to a more natural, healthy way of life. This gradual return to the rural areas has helped to restore interest in our country churches and more bells now ring out over the moors and marshes than could have been hoped for some years ago.

ST BEUNO
CULBONE, SOMERSET

Culbone church is entered in the Guinness Book of Records as the smallest, complete medieval church still in use in England, measuring 35 feet by 12 feet internally. Its setting is also magnificent, a wooded combe where the hills of Exmoor plunge into the Bristol Channel.

There is no road to Culbone, the only access being by foot along winding tracks that curl down the cliffs through woods and fields.

St Beuno is basically Norman, but most parts have been altered over the years. The nave was re-roofed before 1500, and a thirteenth-century arch replaced the original one in the chancel. A Saxon two-light window is probably the oldest part of the church, and is extraordinary in that it was cut from a single block of stone. The relatively modern spirelet, added in 1810, was made of deal then covered with slate.

The church may be diminutive in size but the pleasure gained from a visit is enormous, a fact reflected in the number of signatures in the visitors' book, despite the long trek.

ST MICHAEL
BRENTOR, DEVON

The view from St Michael's, perched on the summit of an ancient volcanic cone, seems to go on for ever across Dartmoor and the whole southwest peninsula. And when driving in this area, no matter where you are you can see the triangle of Brentor with the church's embattled tower at its apex, for centuries a landmark for sailors returning to Plymouth Sound.

Legends abound as to the origins of the church, one claiming that it was built by a wealthy merchant who, having survived a fierce storm at sea, swore he would build a church on the first piece of land he saw. The present building dates back to the thirteenth century, but mention is made of a church here as early as 1140. St Michael's is plain and primitive, built from the volcanic rock on which it stands, the tower being only about 3 feet from the edge of the precipice. Encircling the cone are earthworks from an Iron Age hill fort.

The church was restored in the late nineteenth century and has a solid granite font in addition to a good modern stained-glass window to St Michael.

ST MARY THE VIRGIN
OARE, SOMERSET

Though Oare is only two miles from the sea, it feels like two hundred since the tiny hamlet is completely surrounded by the wild, round-topped hills of Exmoor. It would probably have remained undiscovered had it not been for R.D. Blackmore's novel, *Lorna Doone*. Set in Oare and the surrounding valleys, the book culminates in the shooting of the heroine at her wedding in St Mary's.

The church has medieval wagon roofs and predominantly Georgian furnishings. In the nineteenth century the tower was rebuilt and the chancel extended. Anyone wishing to reconstruct Carver Doone's foul deed will need to remember that the church originally ended where the screen is now. The shots were fired through one of the single-light windows west of the present screen.

R.D. Blackmore's grandfather was rector of Oare from 1809 to 1842.

ST MARY
TARRANT CRAWFORD, DORSET

An often-muddy farm track is the only way to this interesting twelfth-century church – some windows and the top part of the tower are from later periods. The fields surrounding St Mary's are scattered with flints, a ready source of building material that is evident in the rough flushwork on the walls and tower.

Tarrant Crawford possesses a large collection of quite clearly detailed wall paintings, featuring subjects common to the Middle Ages. The upper half of the nave's south wall is occupied by twelve scenes depicting the life of St Margaret of Antioch, one of the best-loved saints at that time and much portrayed. Her *pièce de résistance* was to emerge unscathed from a dragon's stomach, while making the sign of the Cross. The dragon who swallowed her was, of course, the Devil in disguise.

Another allegory illustrated here is the 'Moral of the Three Living and Three Dead'. A trio of kings with all the trappings of wealth meet up with three skeletons, who warn them against reliance on transitory earthly riches.

CHALBURY CHURCH
DORSET

The tiny hamlet of Chalbury nestles in the gentle Dorset countryside, the church occupying a small hill site on which Saxon and Roman remains have been found. The name Chalbury is derived from the Saxon *Cheoles Byrig*, which means 'Ceol's fort'.

The simple whitewashed church consists of a chancel, nave and south porch, the earliest parts of the building dating back to the thirteenth century. The large three-decker pulpit seems rather out of place in such humble surroundings. Along the south side of the nave are three box pews, which were occupied by the tenants of Chalbury, Didlington and Uppington farms. The raised seat on the north side of the chancel was reserved for the Earl of Pembroke and his family, and the long one on the south side for the rectory servants. The religious snobbery evident in those days somewhat belies the theory that 'all men are equal before God'.

ST MARY
ALMER, DORSET

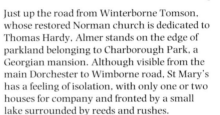

Just up the road from Winterborne Tomson, whose restored Norman church is dedicated to Thomas Hardy, Almer stands on the edge of parkland belonging to Charborough Park, a Georgian mansion. Although visible from the main Dorchester to Wimborne road, St Mary's has a feeling of isolation, with only one or two houses for company and fronted by a small lake surrounded by reeds and rushes.

The church is a mixture of many styles going back to the eleventh century, sadly a great deal of rebuilding has taken place leaving the interior somewhat lacking in atmosphere. Most of the original windows have been enlarged or replaced, but the north window in the chancel has some interesting glass, the centre light being of Swiss origin. Beneath colourful images of John the Baptist, the Virgin Mary and others is an inscription that, when translated, reads, 'The free will is as I to choose between good and evil. Water and fire are put before you, you may seize the one you will.'

A lead-lined twelfth-century font sits on the inverted bowl of another, specially carved and adapted to take it. The churchyard has part of a fifteenth-century cross that once stood near the manor house.

HOLY SEPULCHRE
WARMINGHURST, WEST SUSSEX

The famous Iron Age fort of Chanctonbury Ring can easily be seen from Warminghurst, a remote church set among hop fields and now preserved by the Redundant Churches Fund.

The church is thirteenth-century Early English, remodelled in 1770 when the furnishings were installed. Nave and chancel were then separated by a three-arched screen, above which is a tympanum bearing the colourfully painted coat of arms of Queen Anne. A set of box pews are accompanied by a triple-decker pulpit, all in plain wood and gently lit by the clear-glass lancet windows.

One rather curious item is the wrought-iron crane device used for raising the font canopy. There are several eighteenth-century memorial tablets around the walls and a small brass to Edward Shelley and his nine children. The exterior of Warminghurst church is plain and simple, but has a soft, mellow texture and with its tile-hung bell turret makes an appealing sight, complementing the landscape.

ST MICHAEL
UP MARDEN, WEST SUSSEX

Up Marden church lies 500 feet up on the South Downs, almost totally hidden by trees and tucked away behind farm buildings. Successfully locating St Michael's is well worth the effort, for here is a delightfully unspoilt country church that has not changed since it was built in the thirteenth century.

The outside walls are plastered, and there is a weather-boarded bell chamber although the bells are no longer inside. Two now rest in the chancel, while the third has been mounted outside the south porch so that it may still be used for services.

Perhaps the only jarring note inside is the curiously shaped chancel arch, a seventeenth-century addition needed to support the original. It transpires from the records that complaints were made in 1625 about the condition of the church, not only of the fabric itself but of the general state of the interior. The smell of pigeon dung and other rubbish forced parishioners to 'stop their noses or carry flowers in their hands to prevent the smell thereof'.

ST ANDREW
FORD, WEST SUSSEX

The pretty little eleventh-century church at Ford lies close to the mouth of the River Arun and can only be approached by a field path.

Sandstone and flint have been used for the walls, making an attractively textured combination, and the tiled roof is topped by a dazzling white bellcote. St Andrew's interior is pleasingly simple with a plain Norman chancel arch.

LULLINGTON CHURCH
EAST SUSSEX

Lullington church could possibly be called the smallest in England, but in fact it is only a portion of a chancel. How and when the main body of the original church was destroyed is not known, but it is thought to have happened in Cromwellian times. The dedication is also unknown, one of the few clues being in the will of one Jegelian Hunt, who died in 1521. 'I will a taper sett before St Sithe', he promised, but there is confusion as to whom he was referring. It could have been St Sitha, or indeed, St Osyth, a martyred Saxon princess.

The church was built in the thirteenth century, and was originally a chapel of Alciston. The part that remains has five windows, a piscina, font and single bell. Twenty people can be seated, but at Festivals double that number have squeezed into the 16 foot space.

Lullington is just to the north of Alfriston, an old smuggling village with many medieval buildings.

ST THOMAS THE APOSTLE
HARTY, KENT

If one considers Romney Marsh to be inhospitable and lonely, a visit to the Isle of Sheppey in search of Harty is not recommended. Located in the southeast corner of this bleak Thames Estuary island, St Thomas looks over the River Swale to the north Kent coast.

The moss-covered roof on the north side of the church reaches close to the ground leaving no space for windows, except for one in the small chapel. Ragstone has been used for the walls and the small bellcote is shingled.

For such an isolated church there is a surprising amount of good woodwork; a late-fourteenth-century screen with single, square-headed lights; a chest dated 1375, possibly German, with a carved front showing two knights jousting, their squires in attendance bearing spare lances; an oak table with five sculptured faces; and a minute, hand-turned organ that plays three tunes are some of the absorbing features. Traces of Norman architecture are still visible, notably the arch to the south chapel, which looks as though it has been resited from the chancel. The fabric of the church is mainly from the thirteenth and fourteenth centuries.

ST CLEMENT
OLD ROMNEY, KENT

The rich sheep pastures on which Old Romney sits were once part of the English Channel, clever use of drainage and sea walls over the centuries having left this ancient sea port high and dry.

The church shares its patron saint with four others in Kent. Being so close to the coast it seems a suitable dedication, since St Clement was martyred by drowning in AD 102.

Records show the existence of a Saxon church, but the present one is early Norman, enlarged in the thirteenth century, and the tower added during the fourteenth. This was not built on to the outside of the church, but occupies what was the third bay of the south aisle. Ascent of the tower can be made via a 300-year-old ladder, whose triangular oak steps are sections of diagonally sawn tree trunks.

The interior has a mellow, rural Georgian feeling, emphasized by the box pews and gallery, supported on slender, fluted pillars. All the roof timbers are exposed, the nave roof being carried on huge, rough-adzed cross beams. The Jacobean communion table sits in front of a set of painted boards, still set in their seventeenth-century panelling and depicting the Lord's Prayer, Creed and Commandments.

ST MARY THE VIRGIN
STRETHALL, ESSEX

Strethall is a small, isolated community lost among the farmland of northwest Essex.

The church is mainly Saxon but with a fifteenth-century chancel and tower. Nave and chancel are separated by a finely decorated arch, probably from the time of Edward the Confessor. The nave is Saxon and has good examples of the pre-Conquest long-and-short work on the quoins.

Also of interest is a brass to a priest from the fifteenth-century, the figure being about 2 foot long.

ST MARY
CHICKNEY, ESSEX

One of only a few Essex churches that have visible evidence of Saxon work, Chickney was made redundant in 1974, but has been preserved by the Redundant Churches Fund. The population dwindled over the years making it impossible to keep such a remote church going for a congregation that might number two or three or less.

Nave and chancel are pre-Conquest, although the chancel was extended in the thirteenth century. It is unusual not to find Norman work in such a church, but the architecture jumps from Saxon to Early English. One can easily see the development of window styles through the centuries, starting with the tiny splayed Saxon windows, followed by narrow thirteenth-century lancets and then by larger, two- and three-light examples from the fourteenth century.

Roof timbers inside the church are roughly carved, the marks of the tools being clearly visible. There is a fourteenth-century chancel arch and an elaborately carved font from the fifteenth century. It may take one or two attempts to find St Mary's as it is down a long and winding farm track.

ST MARY

AMPNEY ST MARY, GLOUCESTERSHIRE

There are three Ampneys grouped together a little to the east of Cirencester: St Peter, Ampney Crucis and St Mary. Ampney St Mary differs from its neighbours in that the church is a mile away from the village, quite isolated, with only Ampney Brook and a giant cedar for company.

It has been suggested that the Black Death of 1348 was responsible for the separation of church and community. The village may have been wiped out and then relocated on safer ground.

St Mary's nave dates back to the twelfth century, and the chancel was added later. Perhaps the most striking features of this simple church are the stone rood screen and the remains of extensive wall paintings. The majority of such paintings have long since disappeared under the layers of whitewash that obliterated them after the Reformation, which was also responsible for the disappearance of many fine rood screens throughout the country. St Mary's survived, probably due to its being of stone rather than the usual carved and decorated wood.

ST MARGARET

ST MARGARETS, HEREFORD AND WORCESTER

Hidden away high above the Golden Valley in the tangle of lanes that confusingly links England with the Welsh Marches is the small, two-cell church of St Margaret. Built of rubble and dressed with local sandstone, the simple church is topped with a curious, slightly overhanging boarded bell turret. The atmosphere of peace and tranquillity could be reason enough for visiting this lonely spot, but the interior of St Margaret's is the real joy.

Inside the church is a magnificent, pre-Reformation rood screen and loft, considered to be one of the finest examples surviving today. It was built about 1540 and, miraculously, was not destroyed during the Reformation seven years later when all such works were banned – perhaps because of St Margaret's remoteness.

The carving is quite exquisite and one can only marvel at the skill of those who carried out the work. Oak leaves, vines, fleurs-de-lis, lions and human heads are all perfectly reproduced in the minutest detail. The oldest part of the church is the twelfth-century chancel arch, now partly covered by the screen.

ST MARY AND ST HARDULPH
BREEDON-ON-THE-HILL,
LEICESTERSHIRE

A most dramatically sited church, St Mary and St Hardulph perches precariously close to the sheer stone face of the quarry that has eaten away nearly half of this ancient hill-top site. Archaeological discoveries during quarrying and local building have established that Breedon Hill was an Iron Age fort, traces of the earthworks still being visible to the west of the church.

Breedon is unusual in its dedication, most of the oldest saints being remembered in the church names of Cornwall and Wales, focal points of early Celtic Christianity.

One of the largest collections of Saxon carvings in the country is housed here and Breedon is particularly known for its angel, perhaps the earliest example in any church. Unfortunately it is set in the wall on the first floor of the tower, but the effort required to locate it is well rewarded.

The whole of the north aisle is filled with Shirley monuments and their family pew. This Jacobean monstrosity would originally have been placed in the body of the church, no doubt presenting a daunting sight to the humbler worshippers.

ST MATTHEW
NORMANTON, LEICESTERSHIRE

It is ironic that the *Collins Guide to Parish Churches* should describe St Matthew's as 'sailing like a white ship across the wide green seas of the park'. Prophetic words indeed since the park is now a reservoir and the church does appear to float, but on water not grass.

To preserve St Matthew's from the rising waters the ground level was raised around it and the crypt filled with rubble and sealed with a layer of concrete to just beneath the windows.

Sir Gilbert Heathcote, Lord Mayor of London in 1711. was the owner of the great Palladian mansion at Normanton, a village that he pulled down in 1764 to enlarge his park. The unfortunate inhabitants were transferred to nearby Empingham. The house itself was demolished in the late 1940s leaving the church entirely alone.

The original building dates from 1764 with the Baroque tower being added in 1826. In 1911 the Georgian nave and chancel were replaced with architecture of a similar style to the tower.

Were it not for the £30,000 raised by voluntary subscriptions when the reservoir was made in 1975, Normanton church would have joined the numerous other buildings beneath Rutland Water instead of riding above it.

ST BARTHOLOMEW
LOWESWATER, CUMBRIA

Loweswater is situated on the northwestern edge of the Lake District, where the mountains have a less rugged, more benign appearance. The setting for this small country church could not be more perfect – apart from its neighbour, a sixteenth-century inn, there are only the sheep-covered hills for company.

The religious history of Loweswater extends much further back than the present church, which was not consecrated until 1829. Records at St Bees Priory mention a place of worship here in 1125, but where and for how long is not known. Various incumbents have, through the church registers, recorded fascinating details of life in the fells. The Rev. Thomas Cowper came here in 1744, and stayed fifty-one years. He wrote about the siege of Carlisle by the Young Pretender in 1745, and of assorted natural disasters including 'the greatest storm of wind known to any man living'.

Restoration and alteration were carried out in 1884, resulting in the removal of the three-decker pulpit, box pews and gallery, all of which would be highly prized furnishings today. Sole survivors of the Victorian purge are the painted boards carrying the Creed, Commandments and Lord's Prayer.

CHAPEL LE DALE
NORTH YORKSHIRE

Chapel le Dale is a lonely church sandwiched between two of Yorkshire's highest and most desolate mountains, Whernside and Ingleborough. The church is less than 50 feet long and has an undivided nave and chancel with attractive mullioned windows. Originally built in the seventeenth century, some rebuilding took place in 1869.

Huge beams and king posts are a feature of the interior, which for a moorland church is quite charming. On an inside wall is a sad memorial to the navvies who lost their lives during the building of the Settle to Carlisle railway. One of the great feats of Victorian engineering, the line carved a route through the wild Yorkshire Dales. The most impressive of the many viaducts is Ribblehead, a short way from Chapel le Dale, and it was there that the main shanty town sprang up during the period of building. A bleaker place in winter could not be imagined with terrifying winds screaming up the valley.

NEWLANDS CHURCH
CUMBRIA

There is no village in the Lake District valley of Newlands, the only habitation being the hamlet of Little Town.

The tiny whitewashed church was built to serve an isolated farming community in 1843, and restored in 1885. It has charming round-headed windows, a small gallery and a panelled desk and pulpit, both of which date from the early seventeenth century. There is a schoolroom attached to the church, which has been preserved although no longer in use.

This delightful little chapel, completely surrounded by towering fells, was an inspiration to Wordsworth.

ST PETER
MARTINDALE, CUMBRIA

A narrow winding road follows the lonely, unpopulated south shore of Ullswater before leaving the lake to climb sharply up the fellside by means of tortuous hairpin bends. The church seems to hang precariously at the summit of the climb, surrounded by crags and enjoying a breathtaking view across the lake to the northern fells. At 1,000 feet above sea level this is one of the highest and loneliest churches in England.

The custom of naming many Cumbrian dales after their church's patron saint was followed here in Martindale. St Peter's was not the first church to serve this isolated community, a short distance further on is the original church of St Martin. By the late nineteenth century it had fallen into near dereliction and St Peter's was built to replace it. On the day of consecration, 6 January 1882, a tremendous storm blew the roof off St Martin's. This damage was repaired, but the old church then served only as a mortuary chapel, used for burials.

St Peter's was built in Early English style and has a fine collection of well-designed stained-glass windows, none of which is older than 1975.

ST JOHN THE BAPTIST
EDLINGHAM, NORTHUMBERLAND

Edlingham was one of five villages given to the monks of Lindisfarne by Seowulf, King of Northumbria, who abdicated in AD 737 in order to join the monastery on Holy Island. It is thought there may have been a church here in 740, followed by another in 840, but of these nothing remains.

The stone church that exists now was begun in 1050, the tower and north aisle being added later. The tower has a no-nonsense defensive look, square and solid with slit windows. One of the earlier parts of the church is the south porch, whose tunnel vault is most unusual for early Norman architecture. The chancel arch has decoration of a more familiar kind, roll moulding surrounded by a rectangular-patterned frieze.

Close to the church is the ruin of a fourteenth-century castle, which is undergoing excavation. Judging by what is visible, it must have been an outstanding example. Sir William de Felton, an owner of the castle in the fourteenth century, is buried inside the church.

MATTERDALE CHURCH
CUMBRIA

Matterdale was once part of the parish of Greystoke, whose church was made collegiate in 1382. The undedicated church, set among lonely fells, was the outcome of petitions made by local inhabitants who were gravely concerned by their distance from the Mother church. The consecration of Matterdale was made by Bishop Meye in 1580 after acknowledging that 'their parish church of Greystoke is so far distant from them, and from the annoyances of snow or other foul weather in the winter season in that fellish part, they be often very sore troubled with carrying the dead corpses within the said chapelry and the infants there born unto burial and christening to their said parish church of Greystoke.' The chapel was then licensed for baptisms, marriages and burials.

A huge beam in the church bears the date 1573, the likely year of completion of the building. In 1750 the floor was flagged and seating replaced, having rotted on the bare earth floor. The rather quaint tower was rebuilt in 1848 when the thatched roof was replaced by the slates that exist today.

ST MARY THE VIRGIN
LINDISFARNE OR HOLY ISLAND, NORTHUMBERLAND

High tide floods the causeway that links Lindisfarne to the Northumbrian coast, so careful study of the tide tables is advised before crossing to avoid an unscheduled overnight stop. Driving across the sand-swept road seems to take one back through the centuries, to the time of St Aidan who sailed from Iona to bring Celtic Christianity to the wild north, and to the time of the Lindisfarne monks who produced the illuminated Gospels, the originals of which are now in the British Museum.

St Mary the Virgin stands next to the gaunt, skeletal ruins of the eleventh-century Benedictine monastery, which had been built up from the shell of its original buildings after being sacked by the Danes in AD 875. Most of the church is Early English, but the north arcade and chancel arch seem to be Norman, although the arch has been added to with extra masonry for support.

Fishermen attending church traditionally sit in the north aisle, their wives in the nave. St Mary's belfry and single bell were not added until the eighteenth century, the same time as the font with its curious bulbous stem.

Holy Island should ideally be visited in winter to savour the true atmosphere of this remarkable place.

ST FRANCIS
BYRNESS, NORTHUMBERLAND

Virtually the last English habitation on the road that cuts through Redesdale Forest towards the border, this little wayside group of buildings comprises garage, café, hotel and church.

St Francis's was consecrated in 1799 and, as its dimensions are only 29 feet by 18 feet, must be one of the smallest churches in the county. There is nothing pretentious here, a simple country church serving a small community whose livelihood comes from the acres of timber that cover much of this border area. Byrness was formally a chapel under the parish of Elsdon, but has since been established in its own right. Doorways and windows have round heads, the windows filled with Victorian Gothic tracery.

That the church possibly receives a greater number of visitors than could reasonably be expected for its size and location, could be attributed to the fact that the Pennine Way passes right by the door. Byrness is the last sight of civilization before the Way embarks on its final, most testing section, 29 miles across the Cheviot Hills to Scotland.

ALL SAINTS

BROCKHAMPTON-BY-ROSS,
HEREFORD AND WORCESTER

Commissioned by Alice Madeleine Foster in memory of her parents in 1901, All Saints' was designed by William Lethaby and is considered to be a temple to the Arts and Crafts Movement.

The external composition is most unusual having a central tower, short transepts and a tall slender porch tower with a pyramid top. The roof is thatched and the visual impression of the outside of the building is quite extraordinary. Inside the church, the vaults of the chancel and transepts are of limewashed concrete, although the highly original arches are of stone. The interior retains the slightly dark, sombre feeling of the Middle Ages, but any lingering gloom is quickly dispelled by the many artistic features.

The choir stalls contain delicately carved panels in locally grown oak showing forty-eight species of wild flowers and herbs. The stained glass is by Christopher Whall and there are hand-woven tapestries by William Morris from a design by Burne-Jones.

Picturesque is a vastly overused adjective, but its literal meaning, 'fit to be the subject of a striking picture', more than justifies its use here. There can be few English country churches that do not fit that description, whether because the buildings themselves are works of great architectural beauty or because they enhance the landscape of which they are part. What could be more picturesque than a small village whose golden stone cottages are dwarfed by an embattled tower, or a great sweep of landscape from which elegant spires soar above trees and meadows? Seldom in the work of the great English landscape painters is the tower or steeple of a church not an integral part of the carefully balanced composition. Constable's pictures of the Stour valley would somehow be empty without the Perpendicular tower of Dedham rising over the river.

The church is still the focal point of many villages, dominating the houses and cottages that cluster round or radiate from the churchyard. With twentieth-century development often turning villages into small towns, the church plays an important part in keeping the identity of a place alive. Usually wherever the church is there too is the heart of the community, and no amount of modernization can ever sever this link with a historic past.

As the landscape and geology change throughout the country, so do the churches. There are not many places in England where the church is not in harmony with its surroundings – as at Gunwalloe in Cornwall where the low granite church of St Winwalloe crouches on a rolling coastline – and where a clash of colour or texture does occur, the contrast often works to the building's advantage by accentuating features that may otherwise have blended too well into the background. For example, the Victorian church of Baldersby St James, which with its tall spire and red-tiled roof sits prettily in the fields of North Yorkshire.

So varied is the architecture of the English church and the settings into which it has been placed, that any attempt at a definitive list of the most picturesque would be futile, but there are certainly ample visual rewards for anyone who cares to wander the roads of rural England in search of her churches.

ST JUST
ST JUST-IN-ROSELAND, CORNWALL

Roseland has nothing to do with the flower, but is probably derived from the old Cornish word *ros* or *roos*, meaning 'promontory'. It is likely that there has been a church on this site since about AD 550, and although the present one may not be architecturally remarkable its glory comes from the setting. Situated at the head of a tiny creek in the Carrick Roads, opposite Falmouth, the waters almost touch the church walls at high tide.

The heavily wooded churchyard rises so steeply behind the church that the upper lych gate is actually higher than the tower. Many paths radiate up from the church and it is a delight to wander among the tombstones shaded by palm trees, bamboo and rhododendrons.

St Just was drastically and unsympathetically restored during the last century when most of the original furnishings were discarded, although there still remains a beautiful brass of a priest that has been dated to about 1520.

Legend claims that Joseph of Arimathea, a tin merchant, brought the boy Jesus to St Just when on a business voyage to the Fal. It remains a nice thought.

ST WINWALLOE
GUNWALLOE, CORNWALL

Romantically situated by the sea on the lonely west coast of the Lizard peninsula, the church shares its patron saint with several others in the Southwest.

Winwalloe was born in Brittany and founded the 'Church of the Storms' here in the sixth century. Most of the present church belongs to the fourteenth and fifteenth centuries, including a detached tower built into the cliff rock. Major restoration work was required in the nineteenth century after severe storm damage, and the roof is once again in need of attention.

There is the remains of a most attractive screen, made from the wood of a ship, the *St Anthony of Lisbon*, that was wrecked near Church Cove in January 1526. Two of the panels have been restored and show paintings of the Apostles, the style of the work being unmistakably Iberian. The granite high altar was designed by Sir Ninian Comper and the church has two fonts, one early Norman and the other dating from the thirteenth century.

The elements are constantly at work on this exposed coast and cliff erosion threatens ultimately to make St Winwalloe an island church.

ST BARTHOLOMEW
NEWBIGGIN-ON-SEA, NORTHUMBERLAND

North Sea breakers crash perilously close to this dramatically sited church. It stands away from the small town, perched right on the edge of an eroding coastline whose contours are such that St Bartholomew's is almost surrounded on three sides by water. Stout sea defences have hopefully arrested the ocean's relentless advance.

The church's position is made to look even more spectacular by the absence of trees and, a Northumbrian rarity, by its spire. No doubt sailors are happy to have such a landmark but it does rather lack the elegance that has been achieved elsewhere.

St Bartholomew's seems to have been founded in the early thirteenth century, when it consisted of nave, chancel, and north and south aisles. Later in the same century a tower was added and, judging by the wider arches, the arcades lengthened. The spire was built in the fourteenth century. The chancel retains its original windows: three- and five-light lancets, and a larger one with intersected tracery. The pews and floor have been replaced during very recent renovation, but the church has not lost its medieval atmosphere.

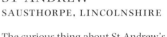

ST ANDREW
SAUSTHORPE, LINCOLNSHIRE

The curious thing about St Andrew's church is its colour. In an area where green sandstone seems to be the most common building material, the sight of a gleaming white spire as one approaches Sausthorpe comes as something of a surprise. Not until one inspects the church closely does it become apparent that this is not a freak limestone building, but is in fact white brick. It must have been a difficult medium to work in, particularly as the tower and spire are highly decorated with turret pinnacles, flying buttresses and other ornamentation.

St Andrew's was designed by Charles Kirk of Sleaford in the mid nineteenth century. Perhaps being a builder as well as an architect enabled him to achieve an end result that, in less capable hands, could have been a visual disaster. The construction is typical of the period: a tall narrow nave and high windows filled with Perpendicular tracery. In the chancel are two William Morris windows.

Sausthorpe is very close to the tiny village of Somersby, birthplace and home of Alfred Lord Tennyson.

ST CYRIAC
LACOCK, WILTSHIRE

Lacock is a picturesque village owned by the National Trust. Houses go back to medieval times and the Trust's attempts to preserve the traditional atmosphere have included piping TV to the community so that no aerials disfigure rooftops and chimney stacks.

Although of Norman origin and unusual dedication, the present church belongs mainly to the fifteenth century, rebuilt from the proceeds of the wool and cloth trade that flourished in this part of England.

The Lady Chapel has a beautiful lierne-vaulted roof and one of the best Renaissance tombs in England for a layman – Sir William Sharrington, first owner of Lacock Abbey after the Dissolution. The relatively little stained glass gives the nave a great feeling of light and space, which helps to accentuate the effect of the barrel-vaulted roof and unusually shaped six-light chancel arch window.

In the south transept is a curious brass dating from 1501, and commemorating Robert Baynard, his wife and no less than eighteen children; all thirteen boys and five girls are neatly lined up below their parents.

Lacock Abbey was the home of William Henry Fox Talbot, pioneer of photography, who is commemorated in the church.

ST MARY
WEST CHILTINGTON, WEST SUSSEX

This twelfth-century church with pretty teak-shingled spire is set in an attractive village near the Sussex Downs. Local stone has been used in its construction, the different colours showing quite clearly through the remains of plastering. Horsham slates cover the large, steeply sloping roof, a style quite common in this region where both nave and aisle are covered by one expanse.

Pride of place in the church has to go to the collection of wall paintings dating from the twelfth to the fifteenth centuries. Many of the images are faded and mere shadows, but more than enough colour and detail remain to allow close study. Perhaps the best illustrations are those from the mid thirteenth century depicting the beginning and end of the life of Christ.

There is also a 'Warning to Sabbath Breakers'. This was a common message and shows Christ being wounded by all manner of work tools instead of by the Centurion's lance, the moral being that if you worked on the Sabbath you were hurting Christ and committing yourself to eternal damnation – evocative and powerful imagery for simple peasants.

ST THOMAS OF CANTERBURY
BRIGHTLING, EAST SUSSEX

Brightling is associated with 'Mad Jack' Fuller who is reputed to be interred within the giant pyramid, seated, wearing a top hat and holding a bottle of claret. It would be fair to say that Fuller was eccentric rather than mad; he built numerous follies in the grounds of his home, Brightling Park, and a 40 foot obelisk on the highest hill in the district.

The church is a mixture of thirteenth- and fourteenth-century architecture, the tower and north chapel being Early English, while most of the windows are in the Decorated style. The fourteenth-century nave has retained its original timber wagon roof. Other features worth noting are the gallery, supported on Roman Doric columns and still containing an old barrel organ, and several brasses, one of which is an elegant portrait of a Thomas Pye.

ST BOTULPH
HARDHAM, WEST SUSSEX

The small rustic church of Hardham is situated on the Arun 'flats' near Pulborough, a little to the north of the Sussex Downs. It dates back to the latter part of the eleventh century and retains some of the original Norman slit windows, although several have been replaced with larger Gothic ones.

St Botulph's simple exterior belies the riches that lie within, for here is one of the most famous collections of early twelfth-century wall paintings. Nave and chancel are covered with these rather faded, but still impressive, examples of early church decoration. There are other churches in Sussex with similar paintings and it is thought that they were all done, or at least influenced, by artists from the great Cluniac priory at Lewes.

Many familiar subjects are depicted: Adam and Eve after the Fall, scenes from the life of Christ, startling comparisons between heaven and hell, St George on horseback. It was not until 1866 that the paintings were discovered, their preservation being largely due to the fact that they are true frescoes, painted on to wet plaster a section at a time.

ST MICHAEL THE ARCHANGEL
PENHURST, EAST SUSSEX

Penhurst derives from the Anglo-Saxon for 'head of the wood', and St Michael's sits high above what must once have been dense, wild forests. The scene today is gentle, the view from the churchyard looking across a valley to the fields and grounds of Ashburnham Deer Park.

The church's setting is idyllic, next to a manor house and a few farm buildings. This is a quiet corner of England at its best. Built from large blocks of Wealden sandstone, the small Perpendicular church has seen little structural alteration since its construction in the late fourteenth century, and although the interior has been scraped, most of the original furnishings remain intact. A fifteenth-century Perpendicular oak screen separates nave and chancel, and while the carved Tudor pulpit may have come from Long Melford in Suffolk, all the box pews were made locally on the Ashburnham estate.

ST GEORGE
TROTTON, WEST SUSSEX

St George's lies close to the medieval bridge that spans the Little Rother river, and is from almost the same period. Largely early fourteenth century, it has the distinction of possessing the oldest brass to a lady in the country, that of Margaret de Camoys, which dates from 1310 and is set in the nave floor. A large table tomb in the centre of the chancel also has a magnificent brass, which is of Thomas, Lord Camoys, one of the English heroes of Agincourt, and his second wife Elizabeth Mortimer, great granddaughter of Edward III. The brass is surrounded by an elaborate border with a canopy over each figure.

The south of England has the lion's share of the best and earliest brasses in the country, probably due to its close proximity to the Continental supplies of latten, a compound of zinc, lead and tin that was used for making the brasses.

Trotton also has well-preserved wall paintings from the fourteenth century, which were uncovered after the removal of plaster in 1904.

ST ANDREW
STEYNING, WEST SUSSEX

Steyning's cottages and buildings form a gloriously coloured jumble from many periods, a mixture of stone, thatch, slate and brick. The church's present dedication was given by the Normans, when they replaced the old Saxon church built by, and named after, St Culman.

Fact and legend are intermingled in Steyning's history. Factual events include the burial here of Alfred the Great's father, in AD 858. While the huge stone slab covered with primitive geometric patterns that now stands in the church porch could be the legendary stone with fantastic healing powers that was associated with St Culman. The name of the village may be based on this story. The Saxon word *Stenningas*, meaning 'the people of the stone', is probably the origin of the name Steyning.

Whatever the truth about this, St Andrew's is a late-Norman church of incredible beauty. The decorative carving in the huge, lofty nave is some of the finest to be found from this period anywhere in England. All the arches and capitals are decorated in elaborate fashion. Rosettes, chevrons, scallops and foliage, the wealth of detail is impressive. The huge flint-and-stone-chequered tower was built in 1600, replacing the earlier central one, but this later addition in no way spoils the appearance of this important church.

ST MARY THE VIRGIN
GREAT BARDFIELD, ESSEX

Great Bardfield and its near neighbour, Finchingfield, are two of the most attractive villages in Essex. Although Great Bardfield has many thatched cottages, the village centre has larger, more impressive half-timbered buildings in company with Georgian shops and houses.

St Mary's stands above the village, next to the timber-framed manor house. The church is mostly fourteenth century, and its greatest feature is the stone rood screen that completely fills the chancel arch. Examples such as this are rare and its presence here in a county that made so much use of timber is even more unusual. The craftsmanship is of a very high standard and it is thought that the screen, which includes the figures of Edward III and his wife Philippa, was erected by Edward Mortimer as a memorial to his wife, who was a granddaughter of the Queen. The Mortimer family are also represented by a stained-glass window dating from 1381, which carries the family's shields.

ST MARY MAGDALENE
MITFORD, NORTHUMBERLAND

Overlooked by a ruined Norman castle, St Mary Magdalene is delightfully situated in the wooded Wansbeck Glen. The church that exists today has seen much rebuilding, due mainly to the effects of a disastrous fire in 1705, which virtually destroyed the nave, the damage not being repaired until a major restoration in 1874.

This was the second big fire in Mitford's history, the first happened just before Christmas in 1215. Having been forced to sign Magna Carta, King John waged a revengeful campaign against the barons. One of them, Roger Bertram, lived at Mitford castle, so it was seized and the church set on fire.

Despite the exterior's modern look, there is a great deal of the past remaining inside. The priest's door on the south side of the chancel is pure Norman, with layers of elaborate decoration. The majority of the chancel was beautifully rebuilt by Adomer de Valance in 1269, exhibiting some of the best features of that period. Particularly good are the six lancet windows running down the south side. Parts of the nave have retained their Norman work, notably the south arcade, which consists of three bays of massive stonework.

ST JOHN THE BAPTIST
LITTLE MAPLESTEAD, ESSEX

Four round churches remain in use in England today: two are associated with the Knights Hospitallers and Templars. Little Maplestead belonged to the former. These military religious orders originated during the Crusades, their round churches being based on the church of the Holy Sepulchre in Jerusalem.

The Hospitallers were formed in 1092 with the founding of a hospice in Jerusalem for pilgrims visiting the Holy Land. The St John Ambulance Association is a direct descendant of the Hospitallers, who fled to Malta after the Reformation but later returned to revive the order here in the nineteenth century.

St John the Baptist's was built in 1340 and supersedes an earlier church. It consists of a spacious chancel ending in a rounded apse, and a hexagonal nave that is separated from the circular aisle by attractive, well-proportioned arcading. The church is topped by a low belfry and entered through a rather unattractive modern porch.

At one time a solid screen separated nave and chancel, ensuring privacy for the Knights who conducted their own services as prescribed by the Order. This probably meant that the nave was for parochial use, and explains why St John's survived the Dissolution when the hospital and associated buildings were pulled down.

ALL SAINTS
HILLESDEN, BUCKINGHAMSHIRE

The road goes no further than this tiny village and at its end stands a magnificent Perpendicular church, one of the best examples in the county.

During the Civil War Hillesden was a Royalist stronghold, the home of the Denton family whose mansion was razed to the ground after fierce fighting, bullet marks from which can still be seen on the church walls. The Dentons are remembered in All Saints' by several monuments and their presence explains why such an impressive church is located in this isolated place.

Built in the late fifteenth century, crenellations run round the walls and there is an intriguing two-storey vestry with a turret, topped by an elaborately pinnacled crown. Clerestory windows of clear glass flood the interior with light. Elsewhere in the church early-sixteenth-century stained glass of a rare quality tells the story of St Nicholas in colourful detail.

Round the chancel is a frieze of carved angels bearing scrolls and playing musical instruments. The family pew is ornate and impressive and the two best Denton memorials are those to Thomas in 1560 and Alexander in 1576.

ST CYRIAC
SWAFFHAM PRIOR, CAMBRIDGESHIRE

The delightful village of Swaffham Prior is remarkable in having two churches sharing the same churchyard. They were in fact built for separate parishes, which were amalgamated in 1667, both buildings being kept in use.

St Cyriac's is now the redundant church, its neighbour St Mary's fulfilling the needs of the modern parish. Both have unusual towers. St Mary's has a fibreglass spire that replaces a stone one, which was damaged by lightning in the eighteenth century. St Cyriac's has a Perpendicular tower with a wonderful octagonal upper stage.

Limestone from the quarries at nearby Reach was used for both churches, St Cyriac's being built during the thirteenth century. It is now almost completely empty apart from a few box pews and a small gallery. Curious pieces of stained glass have been removed to St Mary's, including a picture of Wicken Fen and a portrayal of a First World War trench.

ST MARY THE VIRGIN
UPLEADON, GLOUCESTERSHIRE

Gloriously sited on a clay mound away from the village, Upleadon has one of the best timber towers in the country. This Tudor wood-and-brick structure is unusual in that it rises from ground level with no external support or buttressing, its height accentuated by the closeness of the uprights to each other.

The tower was built on to the Norman twelfth-century nave around 1500. Viewed from the outside it is obviously a separate structure, but the interior has been cleverly incorporated into the body of the church creating a larger nave space. Impressive supporting timbers stretch up into the tower, curving naturally and crossing at ceiling height. Craftsmen's adze marks can easily be seen on the great oak beams, which have been made more durable by recent treatment with epoxy resins. This was just one part of the work required to prevent the total loss of the church, which was declared unsafe in 1966.

Entrance to St Mary's is through a chevron-patterned Norman doorway. The sculptured tympanum depicts the Agnus Dei between two grotesque creatures, no doubt symbolizing the triumph of Christ over worldly evils.

ST MARGARET
BAGENDON, GLOUCESTERSHIRE

A pretty Cotswold village in the Churn Valley, Bagendon's history can be traced to the founding of a tribal capital in AD 10, a huge site bounded by earthworks and encompassing some 200 acres. It was an important centre for trade and industry, especially metalworking, and had a mint for coining silver. Parts of the earthworks can still be traced, and the excavated finds are now displayed at the Corinium museum in Cirencester.

St Margaret's may be of Saxon origin, but the visible evidence is of Norman and later periods. The lower stages of the tower are Norman with a much later saddleback top, a style quite common in this region. A priest's chamber on the first floor has an outside drain leading from a stone basin, and an opening that gives a direct view into the nave.

Most of the windows are now Perpendicular, and some contain good sections of fifteenth-century glass. Identifiable pieces include a skull and feet from an old Crucifix window, a Virgin with outstretched hands, and the patron saint, St Margaret, depicted in red robes.

ST JAMES THE LESS
SULGRAVE, NORTHAMPTONSHIRE

Sulgrave is a place of pilgrimage for many Americans visiting England, as the Manor House was the ancestral home of George Washington. Built by Lawrence Washington in the 1550s, the two-storey grey stone house is now a museum containing many of the President's personal effects.

The medieval church was constructed during the reign of Edward III, a fact commemorated by carvings in the chancel of the King and his Queen, Philippa. A Saxon doorway still remains in the tower, but much of the fabric of the building was altered in the nineteenth century.

As may be expected, there are Washington memorials in the church. Just past the piscina in the south aisle is the seventeenth-century family pew, in front of which and set into the floor is the tomb and brass of Lawrence and his wife Amee. The Elizabethan glass window directly in front of the pew depicts the coats of arms of three generations of the family, all showing the mullets and bars that inspired the Stars and Stripes.

ST HELEN AND THE HOLY CROSS
SHERIFF HUTTON, NORTH YORKSHIRE

Sheriff Hutton occupies an elevated position overlooking the Howardian Hills, the towers of York Minster being visible on the skyline some nine miles away. The clatter of thoroughbred horses' hooves echo round the village, which is part of the North's main racing centre, based on Malton.

Dramatic ruins of a fourteenth-century castle soar above the brick and stone cottages that line a gently sloping road down to the church. A mixture of limestone and sandstone gives this building a warm, golden look, and also indicates where repairs and additions have been made at different times. The lower section of the tower is the oldest part of the church, probably late Norman, the rest originating from the fourteenth and fifteenth centuries.

Two chapels were added to the north- and southeast corners, the former containing the best monuments. Buried here and remembered by an alabaster effigy is Edward, Prince of Wales, who died in 1484, aged eleven. He was the son of Richard III, and Sheriff Hutton castle was one of his favourite residences.

Set in the floor near the lectern is another, rather sad memorial, a brass to two babies who died in 1491.

 ST PETER

SOUTH SOMERCOTES, LINCOLNSHIRE

South Somercotes lies among flat green fields interlaced with dykes, just two miles from the sea. The church of St Peter has an elegant fifteenth-century spire that provides a prominent landmark for sailors. Apart from Louth, this is the only spire in the northeastern marshland and St Peter's is known locally as 'Queen of the Marsh'.

The church's interior is unspoilt, reflecting its peaceful surroundings. The Early English arcade has five bays with round pillars and moulded capitals. Chancel, traceried screen and font are all fifteenth century in the Perpendicular style, the font having carved emblems of the Passion.

St Peter's has a notable set of medieval bells, two dating from 1423. The bells are covered with foliage-enriched lettering and grotesques, but despite this the foundry that cast them has not been identified.

ST MARY AND ALL SAINTS

FOTHERINGHAY,
NORTHAMPTONSHIRE

A melancholy, haunting atmosphere seems to pervade the thistle-clad earthworks that are the remains of the castle. It was here, after her imprisonment and trial, that Mary Queen of Scots was executed on 8 February 1587.

Far less sombre is the beautiful church of St Mary and All Saints. Occupying a prominent position above the River Nene, the octagonal lantern tower is a well-known landmark. The collegiate church was erected here in 1411 by Edward, Duke of York, who died at Agincourt four years later. What we see today is a truncated version, the great choir having been demolished in the sixteenth century.

The tall nave is filled with light from the great clear-glass windows. Graceful flying buttresses support the outside walls, built of local Barnack stone. Although light and airy, the interior still has a feeling of austerity, only slightly relieved by some of the fittings. The best of these is undoubtedly the pulpit, restored to its original magnificent colouring in 1967 and bearing the arms of England and France.

ST JAMES
BALDERSBY ST JAMES, NORTH YORKSHIRE

Baldersby St James was designed and built by William Butterfield in 1856, the tiny hamlet consisting of church, vicarage, school and a few red brick cottages. The church was the gift of Viscount Downe of Baldersby Park, built in 1720 – one of the best examples of the Palladian revival in England.

St James's 160 foot spire can be seen for miles across the flat landscape that stretches between the rivers Ure and Swale. A large stone lychgate guards the entrance to the churchyard.

The interior of the church is extremely elegant and quite lavishly decorated. Nave and aisles are of five bays with bands of brick and stone decorating the pillars. Alabaster panelling lines the chancel in which lies a white marble memorial to the Viscount inset with a beautiful gold cross, again by Butterfield who even designed the church plate.

Baldersby St James was considered to be one of Butterfield's most successful projects. It was unfortunate that Viscount Downe died shortly after laying the first stone and never saw his generous gift completed.

ST PAUL
BRANXTON, NORTHUMBERLAND

The countryside around Branxton is beautiful but must be forever tinged with sadness, for this is Flodden. The last great medieval battle to be fought on English soil is remembered by a large monument on the hill overlooking St Paul's. It was here, on 9 September 1513, that a Scottish army led by James IV engaged the English forces under the leadership of Thomas Howard, Earl of Surrey.

It was Henry VIII's invasion of France that caused James to march, having recently renewed the 'Auld Alliance' with that country. The actual fighting lasted for about two hours, in which time such slaughter took place that the mind finds it hard to cope with the horror of the statistics.

About 9,000 Scots were slain, including the King and almost the entire ruling class. English casualties were much lighter, but the total loss of life was horrendous. King James's mutilated body was laid in St Paul's chancel overnight before being taken to Berwick for embalming.

There has been a church here since the twelfth century, although the present building is virtually a reconstruction done in 1849. Of the original fabric only the chancel arch and supports remain.

ST MICHAEL
STINSFORD, DORSET

St Michael's church is perhaps best known as being the burial place of Thomas Hardy or, to be more precise, one of two final resting places. His ashes lie in Westminster Abbey, the grave at Stinsford contains only his heart. Hardy rests alongside many other members of the family, who are commemorated by a plaque inside the church for forty years' service in the choir.

The church is essentially Early English with a fourteenth-century tower, now devoid of pinnacles and battlements. There may have been an earlier church on this site as a Norman font of Purbeck marble was unearthed in the churchyard. Despite being broken into seven pieces, it has been so carefully reconstructed that it is still used today.

There is a most attractive chancel arch with deep mouldings and the roof has been restored to the original oak, after being hidden by a plaster ceiling for many years. Unfortunately, the wagon roof in the nave has had to be replaced by a less attractive deal one.

Hardy used St Michael's in several of his novels and poems, he referred to it as 'Mellstock Church' and it is beautifully described in *Under the Greenwood Tree*.

ST MARY AND ALL SAINTS
ELLINGHAM, HAMPSHIRE

Situated a little to the west of the New Forest on the River Avon, Ellingham is one of several churches close to the river that possibly occupy the sites of ancient hermit cells, which were often found at crossing points.

The present building dates from the thirteenth century with considerable later additions. Constructed of ironstone and honey-coloured rubble, Ellingham may not be an architectural masterpiece, but is still worthy of note and has many interesting features.

A large, brightly painted sundial sits over the porch, its segments 5 minutes and 35 seconds too small according to the Royal Observatory, who checked it in 1930. Inside the church are an elegant fifteenth-century barrel roof and screen, the space above which is entirely filled with a tympanum carrying a royal coat of arms, the date 1671, the Lord's Prayer, Creed, Decalogue and various texts, all painted and some with Renaissance borders.

The attractive interior is greatly enhanced by the large display of exquisite embroidery. All the pew runners, hassocks and cushions bear work of a very high standard with creative use of design and colour. The work was carried out by members of the church.

ALL SAINTS
WALESBY, LINCOLNSHIRE

Traces of ancient settlements have been found in the vicinity of the village of Walesby, and a Roman villa, covering an area of 100 square yards, was excavated in 1861.

A new church built by Temple Moore in the centre of the village has replaced All Saints', which is now only used for summer services. Located high on a hill it commands panoramic views across the Wolds to Lincoln. There is no road to the church, merely a grassy track. All Saints' was on the verge of ruin before rescue operations began in 1931, but the work has successfully restored this fine building.

Most of the architecture is Transitional to Early English, the gradual change being recognizable from the north to the south arcades of the nave. The chancel dates from the thirteenth century, and retains its priest's doorway and ancient altar stone with five incised crosses.

Some of the furnishings are unusual in that they have been painted white. Particularly impressive is the traceried rood screen and loft. The canopied Jacobean pulpit, also white, came from a Presbyterian chapel at Kirkstead.

ST MARY THE VIRGIN
PAINSWICK, GLOUCESTERSHIRE

The tall, thin spire of St Mary's soars above the centre of this small, attractive Cotswold town. Although quite interesting, the church is somewhat overshadowed by the beauty of its churchyard. Painswick has the most fabulous collection of mainly Georgian table tombs, set among avenues of ninety-nine ancient clipped yews, most of which were planted in 1792.

This collection of monuments not only displays the wealth of the area in the seventeenth and eighteenth centuries due to the wool trade, but also the quality of the locally quarried stone. One particular family of masons, the Bryans, were responsible for a great deal of the work in the graveyard and the church. Painswick quarries supplied most of the stone used for building Gloucester cathedral.

St Mary's is a fourteenth-century replacement of an older church. The tower was added in the fifteenth century, but the spire was not erected until the seventeenth. Fierce fighting took place here during the Civil War in 1644, bullet and cannon shot marks are still evident on the tower and nave walls.

ST GILES
BOWES, COUNTY DURHAM

Bowes gained a degree of infamy by its connection with Charles Dickens's novel, *Nicholas Nickleby*. Dotheboys Hall still exists today, although not as a school. The Academy at Bowes was run by William Shaw, generally thought to be the model for the evil schoolmaster, Wackford Squeers. Shaw himself had been prosecuted for his malpractices, which caused blindness to some of his pupils. The Shaw family are buried in the churchyard of St Giles, which also contains the grave of nineteen-year-old John Ashton Taylor, whose epitaph moved Dickens to create the ill-used boy Smike.

Publication of *Nicholas Nickleby* ruined Shaw and the school was closed. Feeling he had been much maligned, his granddaughter placed a commemorative window in the church in 1896.

St Giles is essentially late medieval with Norman doorways. It has two fonts, one plain Norman with some chevron patterning, the other thirteenth century. The exterior was heavily restored in 1865 when all the pointed lancet windows were put in.

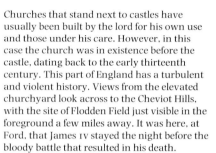

ST MICHAEL AND ALL ANGELS
FORD, NORTHUMBERLAND

Churches that stand next to castles have usually been built by the lord for his own use and those under his care. However, in this case the church was in existence before the castle, dating back to the early thirteenth century. This part of England has a turbulent and violent history. Views from the elevated churchyard look across to the Cheviot Hills, with the site of Flodden Field just visible in the foreground a few miles away. It was here, at Ford, that James IV stayed the night before the bloody battle that resulted in his death.

Both church and castle have been heavily rebuilt and restored, the last major work being done late in the nineteenth century. St Michael and All Angels was greatly altered by John Dobson in 1853 and original sections are few and far between. The south arcade is unchanged, having three wide arches on circular piers with moulded capitals.

Perhaps the outstanding feature is the thirteenth-century bellcote. With space for three bells, although now housing only one, it rises from a strong buttress on the west front and is beautifully shaped in stages up to the pyramid top.

PHOTOGRAPHIC NOTES

One of the chief problems in photographing this collection of English churches was getting a clear view as so many seemed to be hemmed in by trees or surrounded by other buildings. This often meant coming in much closer than I would have liked, resulting in the distortion and converging verticals that are associated with using wide-angle lenses too close to a building.

All my work is done with 35 mm equipment – I used an Olympus OM-2 camera and Kodachrome 25 ASA or Fuji 50 ASA film – so the only way to eliminate the distortion problem was to use a perspective control lens. Although similar to a normal lens in shape and weight, this is constructed in a way that allows part of the lens barrel to move up or down, giving similar control to a large-format technical camera. This facility means that the camera does not need to be tilted in order to get the whole building in and the 'falling over' effect is greatly reduced. Its complex optical arrangement makes the perspective control lens comparatively expensive but it is invaluable for anyone doing a lot of architectural work.

Using the right light is very important to bring out the textures and colours of the stonework, which can look so dull and drab without the sun. Working out which time of day will be best is made easier by the fact that many churches have a south porch and a west tower. If that is the case then the morning is the best time, before the sun swings too far round to the west. Unfortunately the English climate does not always allow one the right conditions, but at least the unpredictable nature of the weather can produce dramatic effects in the sky.

Filters are an essential item and I use them a great deal, not necessarily to change the picture but to enhance what is already there. Blue skies can be darkened by using a polarizing filter, which will increase the drama of the clouds and at the same time reduce reflection from the church windows and roof, allowing greater depth of colour. Graduated filters are useful here for balancing the darkness of a church against a bright sky, enabling both to be correctly exposed without loss of detail.

❧ BIBLIOGRAPHY ❧

Betjeman, John (Ed.) *Collins Guide to Parish Churches of England and Wales*, Collins, 1968; as *Collins Pocket Guide to English Parish Churches* (2 vols), 1976

Blatch, Mervyn *Parish Churches of England*, Blandford Press, 1974; U.S.A. Transatlantic Arts, 1975

Clifton-Taylor, Alec *English Parish Churches as Works of Art*, Batsford, 1974; U.S.A. David & Charles, 1974

Pevsner, Nikolaus *The Buildings of England* (Series), Penguin

INDEX